big**fat**cookies

big**fat**cookies

by elinor**klivans**

photographs by
antonis**achilleos**

CHRONICLE BOOKS
SAN FRANCISCO

Text copyright © 2005 by Elinor Klivans.

Photographs copyright © 2005 by Antonis Achilleos.

Library of Congress Cataloging-in-Publication Data:

Klivans, Elinor.
  Big fat cookies / by Elinor Klivans ; photographs by Antonis Achilleos.
    p. cm.
  Includes index.
  ISBN-13 978-0-8118-4216-7   ISBN-10 0-8118-4216-9
  1. Cookies. I. Title.
  TX772.K5823 2004
  641.8'654—dc22

                            2004005698

Manufactured in China.

Designed by Tracy Sunrize Johnson
Prop styling by Joe Maer
Food styling by Alison Attenbrough

Distributed in Canada by Raincoast Books
9050 Shaughnessy Street
Vancouver, British Columbia V6P 6E5

10 9 8 7 6 5 4 3

Chronicle Books LLC
85 Second Street
San Francisco, California 94105

www.chroniclebooks.com

dedication

· ·

To **Jeffrey, Laura, Michael, Kate,** and **Peter,**
and our new generation of cookie bakers,
Madison, Charlie, and **Max Jeffrey,**
who share my cookies and make it all sweeter

acknowledgments

Judith Weber, my agent, who makes it all happen.

An exceedingly large thank you to the brilliant publishing group at Chronicle Books, especially:

Bill LeBlond, my editor, who steered this book from its exciting beginnings to its first-class finish.

Amy Treadwell, assistant editor, who took such care with this book at each step of the way.

Judith Sutton, my copy editor, who did such a great job checking everything, and I mean everything, so carefully.

Antonis Achilleos, whose photography captured the spirit of these cookies.

Alison Attenbrough, food stylist, and Joe Maer, prop stylist, who baked the cookies so perfectly and made them look exactly right.

My husband, Jeff, who lived with these cookies, tried every cookie, and never tired of helping me make them better.

My daughter, Laura, who proofread every recipe, made her gleeful corrections, and kept me "hanging in there" with her enthusiastic notes; and my son-in-law, Michael, who gave his thoughtful support, especially about the lemon cookies.

My son, Peter, who despite raising a family, and exams, and moving (several times), somehow kept up with correcting and proofreading every recipe; and my daughter-in-law, Kate, who really loves my cookies.

My mother, who filled my childhood with cookies, and my father, who encouraged it all.

Thank you to the cookie testers who tested many of the recipes: Abby Fitzgerald, Melissa McDaniel, Sue Plaskas, Susan Rockefeller, Dawn Ryan, Louise Shames, Joe Siewers, Kathy Stiefel, and Laura Williams.

A big thank you to my circle of supporters and encouragers: Melanie Barnard, Flo Braker, Sue Chase, Susan Derecskey, Susan Dunning, Natalie and Harvey Dworken, Carole and Woody Emanuel, Barbara Fairchild, Betty and Joe Fleming, Mutzi Frankel, Karen and Michael Good, Kat and Howard Grossman, Helen and Reg Hall, Carolyn and Ted Hoffman, Pam Jensen and Stephen Ross, Kristine Kidd, Alice and Norman Klivans, Dad Klivans, Susan Lasky, Robert Laurence, Rosie and Larry Levitan, Jeanne McManus, Gordon Paine, Joan and Graham Phaup, Janet and Alan Roberts, Louise and Erv Shames, Barbara and Max Steinheimer, Kathy Stiefel, Gail Venuto, Elaine and Wil Wolfson, and Jeffrey Young.

table**of**contents

introduction

● **intro**duction ● ● ● ● ●

Big cookies have always been a part of our family. They have been there to help celebrate our happy times and endure our stressful ones. An Old-Fashioned Iced Molasses Cookie tucked into a lunch box brought a bit of comfort from home on that first day of school. On hectic mornings there were Morning Glory Breakfast Cookies to grab on the way out the door. I have lost count of the boxes of cookies that followed the kids to college. I think baking and sending those cookies soothed my empty-nest blues as much as the children enjoyed getting them. When my husband was teaching our son how to drive, he came home to unwind with his favorite Gingerbread Giants. And when our daughter rented her first apartment, we baked Totally Chocolate Chocolate Chip Cookies. Now that my cookie-baking mother has retired from baking, I send her and dad Vanilla Butter Rounds and Jumbo Almond Elephant Ears. When our son, Peter, married Kate, every guest left with a bag of Big-Hearted Butter Shortbread. The Happy Birthday Oatmeal Cookie became a baby-welcoming cookie when our grandchildren were born.

Measuring milestones, making us feel better, and spreading happiness take very big cookies.

These cookies cover the cookie jar world—in a *big* way. A brief "Taming the Cookie Monster" chapter includes basic cookie making, baking, and storing information. Three recipe chapters follow, which arrange the cookies into chewy, crisp, and sandwich groups. Planning-ahead information is given at the bottom of each recipe, so it is easy to choose the cookies that fit into your time schedule. A quick glance shows the number of cookies that the recipe makes, the time it takes to prepare each batch of cookies, and the baking temperature and approximate baking time. Chocolate Chunk Mountains, Super S'more Crisps, Oatmeal Trailblazers, Chocolate Peppermint Crunch Cookie Bark, Lemon Whoopie Pies—they are all here, ready for lunch bags, after-school snacks, sunny picnics, challenging hikes, soothing of bruises, and making life a whole lot sweeter.

When I told people I was writing a book called *Big Fat Cookies*, every single person had the same reaction. First they smiled, then the smile became a big grin, and then they laughed, quite a bit. If just the thought of a big cookie does that, you can imagine the pure pleasure that baking and eating these cookies brings. I thought that writing this book would be fun. It was. But, somewhere between the Chocolate Chip–Stuffed Cookies and the Super-Fudge Brownie-Drop Ice Cream Sandwiches, I realized that baking the cookies was fun, sharing the cookies was fun, and eating them, of course, was the best part of all. And then, I too smiled, and laughed, and took another bite.

tamingthe**cookie**monster

Cookie making is comfortable and worry free. Mixing, baking, storing—it is all easy. Below are the practical, time-saving ideas and tips that I have found make good cookie after good cookie.

some words about ingredients

COOKIE INGREDIENTS are basic supermarket items, but I have some preferences that work best for me. For example, I use unbleached all-purpose flour. After all, why use a flour that has been bleached to make it whiter? Unbleached flour has an appealing soft, creamy color and it produces great cookies. To control the amount of salt that is added to cookies, use unsalted butter and then add the quantity of salt called for in the recipe. Eggs that are graded large produce a consistent result. For flavorings, use pure vanilla extract, made from vanilla beans, and pure almond extract, which contains oil of bitter almond. I use molasses that is labeled "unsulphured"; the flavor is less strong than sulphured molasses.

ZEST, LEMON, LIME, OR ORANGE, is the rind of the fruit without any of the bitter white pith. Before grating zest, wash the fruit with warm water and dry it. A handy measure to know is that an average-size lemon yields about 3 tablespoons of juice and 2 teaspoons of zest.

THE BASIC RULE FOR CHOCOLATE is to choose a chocolate that tastes good. The ingredients listed on the package for white chocolate should include cocoa butter and those listed for dark chocolate should include chocolate liquor or chocolate: I am not kidding about the listing of chocolate—a poor-quality brand may not include it.

STORE SPICES TIGHTLY COVERED and check that they are fresh by smelling and tasting them. As with chocolate, if a spice tastes good, it will add to the good taste of your cookies.

TASTE NUTS BEFORE USING THEM to check that they are fresh. To toast nuts spread them in a single layer on a baking sheet and bake them in a preheated 325-degree oven. Walnuts and pecans take about 8 minutes; sliced or slivered blanched almonds about 12 minutes, until they become golden; and blanched whole almonds about 15 minutes. Just before the nuts are ready, there will be a pleasant aroma of toasting nuts. Cashew and macadamia nuts are normally sold roasted.

TO TOAST COCONUT, spread it in a thin layer on a baking sheet and bake it in a preheated 300-degree oven for about 10 minutes, or until lightly golden. Stir the coconut once during baking so it toasts evenly.

baking sheets and baking tools

HERE IS GREAT NEWS: all of the cookies in this book are baked on the same type of pan, a baking sheet that measures about 17 by 14 inches. Choose sheets that are heavy and have a shiny finish; you will not be able to bend a heavy baking sheet. Aluminum is a good choice. It has the advantage of having a shiny finish that deflects heat and discourages burned cookie bottoms. Since aluminum absorbs heat evenly, cookies bake evenly. Rather than four sides, baking sheets designed especially for cookies have either curved rims at either end or on one side for grasping the pan. Cookies slide easily off these baking sheets. Baking sheets with 1-inch high sides work fine but usually hold a smaller quantity of cookies. For efficient baking, I recommend buying at least two, and preferably three, baking sheets. Lining baking sheets with parchment paper makes for easy cleanup, cookies that never stick, and eliminates the step of greasing the pans. Rolls of parchment paper are available in supermarkets.

A STANDING ELECTRIC MIXER has the advantage of keeping your hands free during mixing, but a hand-held electric mixer will work fine for any of these cookies. Many new hand-held mixers have beaters with wire spokes rather than those made of flat metal strips; the wire spoke beaters are great at preventing cookie dough from getting caught in the beaters.

MAKING THESE COOKIES really does take very little equipment, but an ice cream scoop with a $^1/_4$-cup capacity makes fast work of making drop cookies, scooping out portions of dough to roll into balls, and making cookies that are uniform in size. And a 12-inch ruler is handy for measuring the thickness of rolled dough and cookie sizes.

mixing cookie dough

MOST COOKIES DOUGHS follow the same mixing pattern. Beat the butter and sugar to blend it smoothly, mix in any melted chocolate, and then add eggs and liquid flavorings. Finally, add the flour or flour mixture and any oatmeal, chocolate chips, fruit, dried fruit, or nuts. That's it. You may notice that when cold eggs are added to some doughs, the batter looks curdled. It happens when the cold egg is combined with the room-temperature butter: what you are actually seeing is small pieces of firm butter. But once the flour is added, any such curdling disappears and the dough looks smooth again.

SOFT CAKE-LIKE COOKIES, such as Pumpkin Butterscotch Chip Cookies, are made with an especially soft dough. Their usual mixing pattern is to beat the eggs and sugar, add oil or melted butter and other liquids, then the flour or flour mixture, and, finally, any butterscotch or chocolate chips, nuts, or dried fruit. There are two other mixing methods used here. For the Almond Butter Crisps with Whipped Chocolate Truffle Filling and the Chocolate Caramel Pecan Clusters, a cooked butter and sugar or sugar mixture is mixed with nuts and flavorings. For the Jumbo Almond Elephant Ears, cold butter pieces are combined with a flour mixture until crumbly, then sour cream is added to form the dough. Other mixing techniques are minor variations on these basic concepts.

forming cookies

THERE ARE SEVERAL WAYS to form these big cookies. One of the most common is the drop method. The batter is simply dropped from a spoon (or ice cream scoop) onto the baking sheet. Another is to roll dough into balls between the palms of your hands, then leave it in balls or flatten it. For the versatile slice-and-bake method, cold logs or slabs of dough are cut into the desired thickness. Some cookie doughs can simply be spread into a large circle and baked; others can be spread on the baking sheet and broken into irregular pieces after baking. Or dough can be formed into a long, thick rectangle and sliced after it is baked. To make cookies with special shapes, the dough is rolled out and cut with cookie cutters or cut with a knife into neat squares or rectangles.

what makes a cookie big

IT IS THE FIRMNESS OF THE DOUGH that makes a cookie hold its shape and not spread all over the baking sheet. Many cookie doughs have a soft but firm consistency that enables them to spread to the desired size. The familiar chocolate chip dough is a good example. A shortbread-type dough is firmer, and it can hold a cut-out pattern when baked. Using cold ingredients for some cookies or chilling a dough can produce a dough good for large cookies. Some cookies, like Chocolate-Covered Chocolate Chip Cookie Mud Balls, are formed from baked cookies. Mix-ins such as oatmeal, nuts, chocolate chips, and dried fruit discourage cookie spreading. Cake-like drop cookies are made from a batter-type dough, but the batter is thick enough to spread. Sandwich cookies, with their two cookies plus a filling, are certainly going to be large, thick cookies.

beautifully baked cookies

"ABOUT" IS THE WORD TO NOTE when timing cookie baking. Ovens vary, temperatures of dough vary, and baking sheets vary. Cookies generally have short baking times, so there is a short window between a perfectly baked cookie and a too-hard or burnt one. The solution is to consider baking times as approximate and to watch cookies carefully during those last few minutes of baking. Checking cookie bottoms by lifting a cookie with a spatula may break one cookie but save the rest of the batch. (You can always eat that broken cookie.)

BAKE COOKIES ON THE MIDDLE RACK OF THE OVEN and at the specified oven temperature. I have found that baking one sheet of cookies at a time produces more evenly baked cookies and eliminates the need to rotate the baking sheets in the oven. Keep in mind that cookies usually bake in less than the specified time if the baking sheet is only partially filled. And if reusing a baking sheet, let it cool before adding more cookies. Cool cookies on wire racks to allow for air circulation that will keep them crisp.

baking ahead: storing and freezing cookies

IF PROPERLY WRAPPED, most cookies can be stored perfectly for at least three days after they are baked, and some cookies, like Gingerbread Giants, keep well for as long as three weeks. The best way to store chewy cookies is sealed tightly in a plastic container or tin. For crisp cookies, a tin works better than a plastic container. Tightly closed containers protect cookies from odors and humidity. Each type of cookie should be in its own container so the cookies do not take on the flavor of others. It's a good idea to put a layer of wax paper between each layer of cookies. If cookies have a perishable frosting or filling, refrigerate them after covering them or putting them in a covered container. Most other cookies are fine stored at room temperature.

Properly wrapped, most cookies can be frozen for up to three months. It's usually best to wrap each cookie in plastic wrap before putting it in a plastic container or tin, but if the cookies are not sticky, two or three can be wrapped together. This wrapping only takes a few minutes and prevents any possibility of "freezer taste" by protecting the cookies from the air trapped in the container. Then take out as many cookies from the container as you need, and be sure to defrost them still wrapped, so any moisture that forms is on the wrapper, not the cookie.

have cookie, will travel

I AM A SECOND-GENERATION COOKIE MAILER. My mom always sent cookies to anyone in the family who was away from home or who she thought needed a cookie pick-me-up. Mailing someone a box of cookies was her way and is now my way of sending good wishes, congratulations, encouragement, gifts, a thank-you, or just a bit of happiness. My baking friend Dawn Ryan keeps in touch with a "cookie of the month" list. Her lucky faraway friends and family receive a box of cookies each month.

When shipping cookies, choose those that have a good shelf life and are normally stored at room temperature. Hold back on mailing cookies with chocolate fillings or toppings until cool weather arrives. Good packaging is the key to having cookies arrive in good condition. First put a layer of crumpled wax paper in a rigid plastic container or metal tin. This will cushion the cookies. Then fill the container with individually wrapped cookies. Gift-wrap the container, if you like. Wrap the container heavily in brown paper or newspaper and pack it in a carton with packing material surrounding it on all sides. A large carton can hold several containers of cookies. It is a good idea to ship cookies either early in the week or by overnight delivery so they do not spend the weekend in a warehouse somewhere.

big cookie ideas

BIG COOKIES CAN BECOME DESSERT for an informal occasion or a grand party. On the simplest level, there is ice cream and cookies or just a plate of assorted cookies. Take it a step further and make ice cream sandwiches. Chocolate chip or chocolate cookies can serve as the base for a sundae. Top each cookie with a scoop of ice cream and cover it with hot fudge sauce. Or make a cookies and cream parfait by filling goblets with layers of cookie pieces, ice cream, and sauce. Moving on to "grander" ideas, short-bread or vanilla butter cookies can be heaped with fresh berries and whipped cream. Cookie trifles are party fare: Layer cookies with appropriate flavors of whipped cream in a large glass bowl. Crumble a cookie or two over the top layer of whipped cream, sprinkle with powdered sugar, and dig in. Try pairing spice cookies with cinnamon whipped cream; chocolate cookies or oatmeal cookies with vanilla, coffee, or chocolate whipped cream; and shortbread, vanilla cookies, or pecan cookies with raspberry or rum whipped cream. Or put together other flavors that appeal to you to make your own combinations.

big**chewy**cookies

Chocolate chip cookies are probably what come to mind when you think of a big fat cookie. In fact, the first recipe here is for a big chocolate chip cookie made super-scrumptious by means of a method for adding many more chips than usual. But chewy cookies make up a big group. Old-fashioned spice cookies, a giant party-sized oatmeal cookie that serves twelve, cake-like Pumpkin Butterscotch Chip Cookies, big mounded coconut macaroons, and a stunning black-and-white frosted soft cookie are all members of the chewy cookie crowd.

Chewy cookies are formed by several simple methods. Many of them are members of the familiar drop cookie family, made by dropping scoops or spoonfuls of dough onto baking sheets. Several others are made by rolling the dough into balls or logs. Logs of Spiced Walnut-Raisin Hermits are cut into slices after they bake. Chocolate-Covered Chocolate Chip Cookie Mud Balls rely on both methods: baked drop cookies are broken up and then pressed into cookie balls. The dough for A Happy Birthday Oatmeal Cookie is spread into shape.

When deciding whether or not a chewy cookie is done, take the short route: underbaking rather than overbaking is the way to go. If baked a few minutes too long, chewy cookies can dry out and lose their soft texture. Baking them a minute or two less only makes them more chewy.

These are the cookies you want to slip into lunch boxes, pack into picnic baskets, take to a potluck, leave on the counter for any-time-of-day snacks, or send off in the mail. Big City Black-and-Whites and the Chocolate-Covered Chocolate Chip Mud Balls have chocolate toppings and might not travel well during the hot months, but in general, chewy cookies make good shipping choices.

chocolate chip–**stuffed** cookies

Decades of baking chocolate chip cookies have only whetted my appetite for more cookies and more chips. With a layer of chocolate chips baked right into the middle of this thick and chewy chocolate chip cookie, these fall in the "why didn't I think of it before?" great cookie category.

The cookies are made entirely with brown sugar, rather than the usual granulated and brown sugar combination, plus cool butter and cold eggs. This works to produce a cookie dough that is firm and thick enough to hold the middle layer of chips.

2	cups unbleached all-purpose flour
3/4	teaspoon baking soda
1/2	teaspoon salt
1	cup (2 sticks) unsalted butter, slightly softened (for about 30 minutes)
1 1/2	cups packed light brown sugar
2	large cold eggs
2	teaspoons vanilla extract
3	cups (18 ounces) semisweet chocolate chips

Position a rack in the middle of the oven. Preheat the oven to 350 degrees F. Line two baking sheets with parchment paper.

Sift the flour, baking soda, and salt into a medium bowl and set aside. In a large bowl, using an electric mixer on medium speed, beat the butter and brown sugar until smoothly blended, about 1 minute. Stop the mixer and scrape the sides of the bowl as needed during mixing. Add the eggs and vanilla and mix until blended, about 1 minute. The mixture may look slightly curdled. On low speed, add the flour mixture, mixing just until incorporated. Mix in 2 cups of the chocolate chips.

Roll 2 tablespoons of dough between the palms of your hands into a ball, flatten it slightly to make a 2-inch disk, and place on one of the prepared baking sheets Repeat to make a total of 16 disks, placing 8 on each baking sheet and spacing them 4 inches apart. Leaving a $1/4$-inch plain edge, lightly press 1 tablespoon of the remaining chocolate chips onto each disk. Using the remaining dough, make 16 more disks, placing one on top of each chocolate-chip-topped disk. Press the dough disks gently to cover any of the chocolate chip filling that shows around the edges.

recipe continued next page

Bake the cookies one sheet at a time until the edges are lightly browned but the centers are still pale golden, about 15 minutes. Cool the cookies on the baking sheets for 10 minutes, then use a wide metal spatula to transfer the cookies to a wire rack to cool. Serve warm (the filling will be soft and melted) or at room temperature.

The cookies can be stored in a tightly covered container at room temperature for up to 4 days.

choices

Milk chocolate or white chocolate chips can be substituted for the semisweet chips. To serve these cookies for a party, use a large sharp knife to cut the cookies into quarters and dip the pointed ends in Chocolate Coating (page 46). Let the chocolate firm before serving them.

makes 16 cookies ▪ **cookie making** 25 minutes ▪ **cookie baking** 350 degrees, two baking sheets for about 15 minutes each

totally **chocolate** chocolate chip cookies

Twelve cookies, one pound of chocolate chips—sounds like a good ratio to me. For these cookies, some of the chocolate chips are melted and mixed into the dough and some are mixed into the dough as chips. The result is a dark chocolate cookie with a heap of chocolate chips.

2 ²/₃ cups (16 ounces) semisweet chocolate chips
1 cup unbleached all-purpose flour
¼ cup unsweetened Dutch-process cocoa powder
1 teaspoon baking soda
½ teaspoon salt
½ cup (1 stick) unsalted butter, slightly softened (for about 30 minutes)
½ cup packed light brown sugar
¼ cup granulated sugar
1 large cold egg
1 teaspoon vanilla extract

Position a rack in the middle of the oven. Preheat the oven to 325 degrees F. Line two baking sheets with parchment paper.

Put ²/₃ cup (4 ounces) of the chocolate chips in a heatproof container or the top of a double boiler and place it over, but not touching, a saucepan of barely simmering water (or the bottom of the double boiler). Stir the chocolate chips until melted and smooth. Remove from the water and set aside.

Sift the flour, cocoa powder, baking soda, and salt into a medium bowl and set aside. In a large bowl, using an electric mixer on medium speed, beat the butter, brown sugar, and granulated sugar until smoothly blended, about 1 minute. Stop the mixer and scrape the sides of the bowl as needed during mixing. On low speed, mix in the melted chocolate chips until blended. Add the egg and vanilla, mixing until blended, about 1 minute. Add the flour mixture, mixing just until it is incorporated. Mix in the remaining 2 cups chocolate chips.

Using an ice cream scoop or measuring cup with a ¹/₄-cup capacity, scoop mounds of dough onto the prepared baking sheets, spacing the cookies 3 inches apart.

recipe continued next page

Bake the cookies one sheet at a time until they crack slightly on top and a toothpick inserted in the center of a cookie comes out with moist crumbs, not wet batter, about 18 minutes. (If the toothpick penetrates a chocolate chip, test another spot.) Cool the cookies on the baking sheets for 5 minutes, then use a wide metal spatula to transfer them to a wire rack to cool completely. The outsides of the cookies will become crisp as the cookies cool.

The cookies can be stored in a tightly covered container at room temperature for up to 4 days.

makes 12 cookies · **cookie making** 20 minutes · **cookie baking** 325 degrees, two baking sheets for about 18 minutes each

maple cranberry **oatmeal** cookies

Oatmeal cookies that are crisp on the outside and soft on the inside are a classic that never goes out of style. This cookie enhances the perennial favorite with maple syrup and plenty of dried cranberries. It's not too extreme a change—just enough to produce a big sigh of cookie contentment.

1 3/4 cups unbleached all-purpose flour
1/2 teaspoon baking soda
1/4 teaspoon salt
2 teaspoons ground cinnamon
1/2 cup (1 stick) unsalted butter, at room temperature
1 cup packed dark brown sugar
1/3 cup granulated sugar
2 large eggs
1/2 cup maple syrup
2 teaspoons vanilla extract
1 3/4 cups oatmeal (not quick-cooking)
1 1/2 cups dried cranberries

Position a rack in the middle of the oven. Preheat the oven to 350 degrees F. Line two baking sheets with parchment paper.

Sift the flour, baking soda, salt, and cinnamon into a medium bowl and set aside. In a large bowl, using an electric mixer on medium speed, beat the butter, brown sugar, and granulated sugar until smoothly blended, about 1 minute. Stop the mixer and scrape the sides of the bowl as needed during mixing. On low speed, add the eggs, maple syrup, and vanilla and mix until blended, about 1 minute. Mix in the flour mixture to incorporate it. Mix in the oatmeal, then the cranberries.

Using an ice cream scoop or measuring cup with a $1/4$-cup capacity, scoop mounds of dough onto the prepared baking sheets, spacing the cookies at least $2 1/2$ inches apart.

Bake the cookies one sheet at a time until the tops feel firm and the tops and bottoms are lightly browned, about 18 minutes. Cool the cookies on the baking sheets for 5 minutes, then use a wide metal spatula to transfer the cookies to a wire rack to cool completely.

The cookies can be stored in a tightly covered container at room temperature for up to 4 days.

makes 15 cookies · **cookie making** 15 minutes · **cookie baking** 350 degrees, two baking sheets for about 18 minutes each

a **happy birthday** oatmeal cookie

* *

This cookie is ready to party. Chewy in the middle, crisp on the edges, it is a giant cookie—10 inches across—that makes a perfect birthday or anytime celebration "cake" for cookie lovers. Another idea is to use it for sending good wishes in the role of an edible card, with a frosting greeting. Ice cream makes the perfect accompaniment to the wedge–shaped cookie slices. Vanilla, caramel, rum raisin, or butterscotch make particularly good choices.

cookie
1/2	cup plus **2** tablespoons unbleached all-purpose flour
1/4	teaspoon baking powder
1/4	teaspoon baking soda
1/4	teaspoon salt
1/2	teaspoon ground cinnamon
6	tablespoons (3/4 stick) unsalted butter, at room temperature
1/2	cup packed dark brown sugar
1/4	cup granulated sugar
1	large egg
1	teaspoon vanilla extract
1	cup oatmeal (not quick-cooking)
3/4	cup raisins
1/2	cup walnuts, coarsely chopped

frosting
3/4	cup powdered sugar
1/2	teaspoon vanilla extract
3 to 4	teaspoons water

Position a rack in the middle of the oven. Preheat the oven to 350 degrees. Trace a 9-inch circle on a piece of parchment paper and line a baking sheet with the paper, marked side down.

MAKE THE COOKIE. Sift the flour, baking powder, baking soda, salt, and cinnamon into a small bowl and set aside. In a large bowl, using an electric mixer on medium speed, beat the butter, brown sugar, and granulated sugar until smoothly blended, about 1 minute. Stop the mixer and scrape the sides of the bowl as needed during mixing. Add the egg and vanilla and mix until blended, about 30 seconds. On low speed, mix in the flour mixture to incorporate it. Mix in the oatmeal, then mix in the raisins and walnuts.

Drop spoonfuls of dough into the marked circle, then use a thin metal spatula to spread the dough evenly over the circle. Smooth the edges of the circle with the spatula.

Bake the cookie until the edges are light brown and the center is light golden, about 19 minutes. It will spread out about 1 inch. Let the cookie cool completely on the baking sheet on a wire rack.

recipe continued next page

• • • • • • • • • • • • • • • • • • • •

MAKE THE FROSTING. In a small bowl, stir the powdered sugar and vanilla together with enough water to
form a thick frosting. The frosting should hold its shape
if you drizzle a little on a piece of paper. Spoon the
frosting into a small self-sealing plastic freezer bag.
Press out the excess air and seal the bag. Cut a small
hole in one corner of the bag, about $^1/_{16}$ inch long.

Hold the bag about 1 inch above the cookie at a slight
angle and write your message by twisting the bag and
gently squeezing to release a thin stream of frosting,
moving the bag slowly to form thin letters or a design.
Let the frosting firm at room temperature.

Once the frosting is set, the cookie can be covered and
stored at room temperature for up to 2 days. Use a large
sharp knife to cut the cookie into wedges to serve.

makes 12 large cookie wedges • **cookie making** 20 minutes • **cookie baking** 350 degrees, for about 19 minutes

pumpkin **butterscotch** chip cookies

· ·

Pumpkin gives these soft cake–like cookies a gorgeous golden orange color. Using an ice cream scoop to form the cookies makes the tops nice and smooth. The mounds of batter bake into cookies that look like the smooth, round top of a cupcake.

Because oil is used for the shortening, the batter is especially easy to mix. Line the baking sheets with parchment paper and then butter the paper so the cookies release easily. My friend Dianne Hannan, who shared this recipe with me, sometimes substitutes miniature chocolate chips for the butterscotch chips. Make sure that the label on the can of pumpkin says "pumpkin" rather than "pumpkin pie filling," which has added spices.

2	cups unbleached all-purpose flour
1 1/2	teaspoons baking powder
1	teaspoon baking soda
1/2	teaspoon salt
1	teaspoon ground cinnamon
2	large eggs
1	cup sugar
1/2	cup canola or corn oil
1	cup canned pumpkin
1	teaspoon vanilla extract
1	cup butterscotch chips
	Powdered sugar for dusting

Position a rack in the middle of the oven. Preheat the oven to 325 degrees F. Line two baking sheets with parchment paper and butter the paper.

Stir the flour, baking powder, baking soda, salt, and cinnamon together in a medium bowl and set aside. In a large bowl, using an electric mixer on medium speed, beat the eggs and sugar until smooth and lightened in color, about 1 minute. Stop the mixer and scrape the sides of the bowl as needed during mixing. On low speed, mix in the oil, pumpkin, and vanilla until blended. Mix in the flour mixture to incorporate it. Mix in the butterscotch chips.

Using an ice cream scoop with a $1/4$-cup capacity, scoop mounds of the dough onto the prepared baking sheets, spacing the cookies at least 2 $1/2$ inches apart. Or use a measuring cup with a $1/4$-cup capacity to scoop out the mounds of dough, then use a thin metal spatula to smooth the mounds.

Bake the cookies one sheet at a time until the tops feel firm and a toothpick inserted in the center comes out dry, about 16 minutes. Cool them on the baking sheets for 5 minutes, then use a wide metal spatula to transfer the cookies to a wire rack to cool completely.

Dust the cooled cookies lightly with powdered sugar. The cookies can be stored in a tightly covered container at room temperature for up to 4 days.

makes 14 cookies · **cookie making** 15 minutes · **cookie baking** 325 degrees, two baking sheets for about 16 minutes each

old-fashioned **iced molasses** cookies

• •

These cozy spice cookies, which have a soft texture, a dark golden color, and a good but not overly strong molasses flavor, are not for summer. Save them for warming up a fall morning, winter evening, or wet spring afternoon.

cookies

- **2** cups unbleached all-purpose flour
- **1** teaspoon baking soda
- **1/4** teaspoon salt
- **1** teaspoon ground ginger
- **1** teaspoon ground cinnamon
- **1/4** teaspoon ground cloves
- **6** tablespoons (3/4 stick) unsalted butter, at room temperature
- **6** tablespoons vegetable shortening, such as Crisco
- **1** cup sugar
- **1** large egg
- **1/4** cup unsulphured molasses
- **1/2** cup sour cream

icing

- **1** cup powdered sugar
- **1/2** teaspoon vanilla extract
- **2** tablespoons milk, plus up to **1** teaspoon if needed

MAKE THE COOKIES. Sift the flour, baking soda, salt, ginger, cinnamon, and cloves into a medium bowl and set aside. In a large bowl, using an electric mixer on medium speed, beat the butter, shortening, and sugar until blended, about 1 minute. Stop the mixer and scrape the sides of the bowl as needed during mixing. Add the egg, molasses, and sour cream and mix until blended and the color is an even light brown, about 1 minute. (At first the mixture may look separated and multicolored, but it will become evenly colored.) On low speed, add the flour mixture, mixing just until the flour is incorporated and a soft, sticky dough forms. Cover the bowl and chill until the dough is firm enough to form into balls, about 2 hours.

Position a rack in the middle of the oven. Preheat the oven to 350 degrees F. Line a baking sheet with parchment paper.

For each cookie, use an ice cream scoop or measuring cup with $^1/_4$-cup capacity to portion the dough, then roll each one between the palms of your hands into a ball. Place the cookies on the prepared baking sheet, spacing them 3 inches apart. Bake until the tops feel firm but the centers still feel soft, there are small cracks on top, and the bottoms are slightly browned, about 18 minutes. Cool the cookies on the baking sheets for 5 minutes, then use a wide metal spatula to transfer the cookies to a wire rack to cool completely.

MAKE THE ICING. In a small bowl, stir the powdered sugar and vanilla together with enough milk to form a thick frosting. Use a small spoon to drizzle the icing over each cookie. Let the cookies sit at room temperature until the icing is firm.

The cookies can be stored in a tightly covered container at room temperature for up to 4 days.

makes 12 cookies • **cookie making** 20 minutes • **cookie baking** 350 degrees, for about 18 minutes

chocolate chip cookies **in a cookie**

....

Calling all crisp chocolate chip cookie lovers. Calling all soft, chewy chocolate chip cookie lovers. This twice-baked cookie is for both. The cookie starts with a bowl of chocolate chip cookie dough. Some of the dough is baked into crisp cookies, which are then mixed into the remaining unbaked dough and baked together. The result is a soft and chewy cookie with crisp pieces of cookie throughout. Yes, it is as good as it sounds.

If you have some baked chocolate chip cookies on hand, they can be mixed into any chocolate chip cookie dough. A good proportion is about 1 cup of baked chocolate chip cookie pieces for every 2 cups of dough, but a little more or less is fine.

2 cups unbleached all-purpose flour
1 teaspoon baking soda
1/2 teaspoon salt
1 cup (2 sticks) unsalted butter, at room temperature
1 cup packed light brown sugar
1/2 cup granulated sugar
2 large eggs
2 teaspoons vanilla extract
3 cups (18 ounces) semisweet chocolate chips

Position a rack in the middle of the oven. Preheat the oven to 350 degrees F. Line two baking sheets with parchment paper. (One sheet will be used first, then cooled, relined, and used again.)

Sift the flour, baking soda, and salt into a medium bowl and set aside. In a large bowl, using an electric mixer on medium speed, beat the butter, brown sugar, and granulated sugar until smoothly blended, about 1 minute. Stop the mixer and scrape the sides of the bowl as needed during mixing. Add the eggs and vanilla and mix until blended, about 1 minute. On low speed, add the flour mixture, mixing just until it is incorporated. Mix in the chocolate chips.

Drop 10 heaping tablespoons (about 3 level tablespoons each) of dough 3 inches apart onto one of the prepared baking sheets. Set the remaining dough aside. Bake until the edges of the cookies are lightly browned but the centers are still golden, about 13 minutes. Cool the cookies on the baking sheet for 5 minutes, then use a wide metal spatula to transfer the cookies to a wire rack to cool completely. (Leave the oven on.) Line the baking sheet with a clean piece of parchment paper.

Break the cooled cookies into $^1/_2$- to 1-inch pieces. Add the pieces to the reserved dough and mix on low speed just to distribute them evenly, about 10 seconds. Using an ice cream scoop or measuring cup with a $^1/_4$-cup capacity, scoop mounds of dough onto the prepared baking sheets, spacing the cookies 3 inches apart.

Bake the cookies one sheet at a time until they feel firm on the top but are still soft in the center and the edges are beginning to brown slightly, about 15 minutes. Cool the cookies on the baking sheets for 10 minutes, then use a wide metal spatula to transfer them to a wire rack to cool completely.

The cookies can be stored in a tightly covered container at room temperature for up to 4 days.

makes 20 cookies • **cookie making** 25 minutes
cookie baking 350 degrees, one baking sheet for about 13 minutes, then two baking sheets for about 15 minutes each

butterscotch marble **blondie** drops

Even butterscotch blondie brownies can become cookies. Simply drop this blondie batter onto a cookie sheet to produce brown sugar butterscotch cookies with a soft center and super crisp edges. I did gild the lily, actually the cookie, by swirling melted chocolate into each cookie before baking it.

4 ounces semisweet chocolate, chopped
2 cups unbleached all-purpose flour
1 teaspoon baking powder
1/4 teaspoon salt
1 cup (2 sticks) unsalted butter, at room temperature
2 cups packed light brown sugar
2 teaspoons vanilla extract
3 large eggs

Position a rack in the middle of the oven. Preheat the oven to 350 degrees F. Line two baking sheets with parchment paper.

Put the chocolate in a heatproof container or the top of a double boiler, and place it over, but not touching, a saucepan of barely simmering water (or the bottom of the double boiler). Stir the chocolate until it is melted and smooth. Remove from the water and set aside.

Sift the flour, baking powder, and salt into a medium bowl and set aside. In a large bowl, using an electric mixer on medium speed, beat the butter, brown sugar, and vanilla until smoothly blended, about 1 minute. Stop the mixer and scrape the sides of the bowl as needed during mixing. Add the eggs and mix until blended, about 1 minute. On low speed, add the flour mixture, mixing just until it is incorporated.

Drop heaping tablespoons (about 3 level tablespoons each) of dough 3 inches apart onto the prepared baking sheets. Drizzle about $1/2$ teaspoon of the melted chocolate over the top of each cookie. Using a small sharp knife, gently swirl the chocolate once or twice through the cookie to marbleize it.

Bake the cookies one sheet at a time until the tops feel soft but set and the edges are lightly browned, about 11 minutes. Cool the cookies on the baking sheets for 10 minutes, then use a wide metal spatula to transfer them to a wire rack to cool completely.

The cookies can be stored in a tightly covered container at room temperature for up to 4 days.

makes 24 cookies · **cookie making** 15 minutes · **cookie baking** 350 degrees, two baking sheets for about 11 minutes each

chocolate-covered **chocolate chip cookie** mud balls

Making these cookies will take you back to childhood mud pie—making days. The cookie balls are formed by quickly breaking up warm chocolate chip cookies, pressing them into balls, and refrigerating them until firm; the soft chocolate chips hold the cookies together until chilling firms them. That is the mud pie stage. Then they are dipped in melted chocolate. That is the gorgeous stage.

cookies

1	cup unbleached all-purpose flour
1/2	teaspoon baking soda
1/4	teaspoon salt
1/2	cup (1 stick) unsalted butter, at room temperature
1/2	cup packed light brown sugar
1/4	cup granulated sugar
1	large egg
1	teaspoon vanilla extract
1	cup (6 ounces) semisweet chocolate chips

chocolate coating

2	cups (12 ounces) semisweet chocolate chips, chopped
1	ounce unsweetened chocolate, chopped
3	tablespoons canola or corn oil

Position a rack in the middle of the oven. Preheat the oven to 350 degrees F. Line a baking sheet with parchment paper.

MAKE THE COOKIES. Sift the flour, baking soda, and salt into a small bowl and set aside. In a large bowl, using an electric mixer on medium speed, beat the butter, brown sugar and granulated sugar until smoothly blended, about 1 minute. Stop the mixer and scrape the sides of the bowl as needed during mixing. Mix in the egg and vanilla until blended, about 1 minute. The mixture may look slightly curdled. On low speed, add the flour mixture, mixing just until it is incorporated. Mix in the chocolate chips.

Drop heaping tablespoons (about 3 level tablespoons each) of dough 3 inches apart onto the prepared baking sheet, to make 12 cookies. Bake until the edges are lightly browned but the centers are still pale golden, about 14 minutes.

If any of the cookies spread together, use a small knife to cut the warm cookies apart. Cool the cookies on the baking sheet on a wire rack for about 20 minutes, or just until they are cool enough to handle comfortably and break apart.

Line a platter with parchment or wax paper. Break a cookie into $1/2$- to 1-inch pieces and use your hands to press it together into a ball. (The melted chocolate chips will hold the cookie ball together.) Place the cookie ball on the paper-lined platter, and continue to make the rest of the cookies into balls. Cover and refrigerate the cookies until firm, at least 25 minutes, or overnight.

MAKE THE CHOCOLATE COATING. Put both chocolates and the oil in a heatproof container or the top of a double boiler and place it over, but not touching, a saucepan of barely simmering water (or the bottom of the double boiler). Stir until the chocolate is melted and smooth. Scrape the chocolate coating into a medium bowl and let it sit for about 10 minutes to cool and thicken slightly.

Dip a chilled cookie ball in the chocolate and gently roll it around to coat thoroughly. With your fingers, hold the cookie over the bowl to let any excess drip off, then return the cookie to the paper-lined platter. Repeat to dip all of the cookies; do not let the coated cookies touch one another. (You will have some chocolate coating left over for another use or to pour over ice cream; working with a larger quantity of chocolate coating makes for easier dipping.)

Let the cookies sit at room temperature until the chocolate coating is firm, about 1 hour. Or, to speed the firming of the chocolate, refrigerate the cookies for about 15 minutes. A small flat chocolate "foot" will form on the bottom of each cookie.

The cookies can be individually wrapped in plastic wrap and stored in the refrigerator for up to 5 days. Serve at room temperature.

choices

Drizzle the chocolate-coated cookies with thin lines of melted white chocolate. Or cut the cookie into quarters and serve as mud ball wedges.

makes 12 cookies • **cookie making** 25 minutes plus chilling time • **cookie baking** 350 degrees, for about 14 minutes

spiced **walnut-raisin** hermits

· ·

"Don't change a thing, they are perfect," exclaimed my daughter, Laura, when she tasted these spice cookies that are
crisp on the outside and moist and chewy on the inside. Laura knows my tendency to keep baking and changing recipes,
but she was right, I didn't change a thing.

cookies

2	cups unbleached all-purpose flour
1 1/2	teaspoons baking soda
1/4	teaspoon salt
2	teaspoons ground cinnamon
1	teaspoon ground ginger
1/2	teaspoon ground cloves
1/2	cup (1 stick) unsalted butter, at room temperature
1	cup packed light brown sugar
1	large egg
2	tablespoons unsulphured molasses
1	cup raisins
1/2	cup walnuts, coarsely chopped

icing

1/2	cup powdered sugar
3 to 4	teaspoons milk

Position a rack in the middle of the oven. Preheat the oven to 350 degrees F. Line a baking sheet with parchment paper.

MAKE THE COOKIES. Sift the flour, baking soda, salt, cinnamon, ginger, and cloves into a medium bowl and set aside. In a large bowl, using an electric mixer on medium speed, beat the butter and brown sugar until blended, about 1 minute. Stop the mixer and scrape the sides of the bowl as needed during mixing. Add the egg and mix until blended, about 30 seconds. On low speed, mix in the molasses. Add the flour mixture, mixing just until it is incorporated. Mix in the raisins and walnuts.

Divide the dough in half and form it into 2 logs. Place the logs 3 inches apart on the prepared baking sheet, and pat each into an 11-by-2 1/2-by-1-inch-thick rectangle. Bake until the tops feel crusty but the interior feels soft when gently pressed, about 15 minutes; the edges will have just begun to brown.

Cool the logs on the baking sheets for 10 minutes, then use a wide metal spatula to transfer them to a wire rack to cool completely. Cut each cooled log into 6 pieces about 2 inches wide.

MAKE THE ICING. In a small bowl, stir the powdered sugar together with enough milk to form a thick but pourable icing. Use a small spoon to drizzle several thin lines of icing over each cookie. Let the cookies sit at room temperature until the icing is firm.

The cookies can be stored in a tightly covered container at room temperature for up to 5 days.

makes 12 cookies · **cookie making** 15 minutes · **cookie baking** 350 degrees, for about 15 minutes

cranberry-walnut cream cheese **cookie mounds**

• •

This is the story of the birth of a cookie: My best "cookie friend," Dawn Ryan, mailed me her favorite store-bought cookie with a plea to figure out how to reproduce them. When I tasted the cinnamon cookie loaded with fruits and nuts, they reminded me of rugelach. I was off and baking. The recipe grew over months of testing, e-mails, and sample mailings. Finally, Dawn pronounced them "perfect, terrific, and a keeper."

Although the same amount of dried cranberries can be used in a pinch, fresh cranberries give the best result.

cookies

1	cup plus **2** tablespoons unbleached all-purpose flour
1/3	cup sugar
1 1/2	teaspoons ground cinnamon
1/8	teaspoon salt
1/2	teaspoon baking powder
4	ounces cream cheese, cut into 4 pieces, at room temperature
1/2	cup (1 stick) cold unsalted butter, cut into 3/4-inch pieces
2	tablespoons sour cream
1 1/2	teaspoons vanilla extract
1/3	cup dried currants
1/4	cup golden raisins
1	cup finely chopped walnuts
1/3	cup coarsely chopped fresh or defrosted frozen cranberries

glaze

3/4	cup powdered sugar
1/4	teaspoon vanilla extract
4 to 5	teaspoons water

Position a rack in the middle of the oven. Preheat the oven to 350 degrees F. Line a baking sheet with parchment paper.

MAKE THE COOKIES. In a large bowl, using an electric mixer on low speed, combine the flour, sugar, cinnamon, salt, and baking powder. Add the cream cheese and butter, mixing until large clumps of dough form. Stop the mixer and scrape the sides of the bowl as needed during mixing. Mix in the sour cream and vanilla just to blend and form a soft dough. Stir in the currants, raisins, walnuts, and cranberries.

Use an ice cream scoop with a $1/4$-cup capacity to scoop out balls and place them about $1 1/2$ inches apart on the prepared baking sheet. Or use your hands to roll $1/4$-cup portions of dough into balls.

Bake until the bottoms are lightly browned and the tops feel firm, about 25 minutes. Cool on the baking sheet for 5 minutes, then use a wide metal spatula to transfer the cookies to a wire rack to cool completely.

GLAZE THE COOKIES. In a small bowl, mix the powdered sugar, and vanilla with enough water to make a thick but pourable glaze. Drizzle the glaze over the tops of the cooled cookies. Let the cookies sit at room temperature until the glaze is firm.

The cookies can be stored in a tightly covered container at room temperature for up to 4 days.

makes 10 cookies • **cookie making** 20 minutes • **cookie baking** 350 degrees, for about 25 minutes

super-sized **ginger** chewies

My daughter has a friend, Joe Siewers, whose mother, Betty, makes the best strawberry jam I have ever tasted. So it came as no surprise that her ginger cookie recipe turned out to be this perfect example of a thick, chewy spice cookie. Rolling the cookies in sugar before they are baked makes the outsides especially crisp and a good contrast to the soft interior.

2 1/4	cups unbleached all-purpose flour
2	teaspoons baking soda
1/4	teaspoon salt
1	teaspoon ground cinnamon
1	teaspoon ground ginger
1/2	teaspoon cloves
3/4	cup (1 1/2 sticks) unsalted butter, at room temperature
1	cup packed light brown sugar
1	large egg
1/4	cup molasses
about 1/4	cup granulated sugar

Position a rack in the middle of the oven. Preheat the oven to 350 degrees F. Line two baking sheets with parchment paper.

Sift the flour, baking soda, salt, cinnamon, ginger, and cloves into a medium bowl and set aside. In a large bowl, using an electric mixer on medium speed, beat the butter and brown sugar until smoothly blended, about 1 minute. Stop the mixer and scrape the sides of the bowl as needed during mixing. Add the egg and molasses and mix until blended and an even light brown color, about 1 minute. On low speed, add the flour mixture, mixing just to incorporate it.

Spread the granulated sugar on a large piece of wax or parchment paper. Roll $^1/_4$ cup of dough between the palms of your hands into a 2-inch ball, roll the ball in the sugar, and place on one of the prepared baking sheets. Continue making cookies, spacing them 2 inches apart.

Bake the cookies one sheet at a time until the tops feel firm but they are still soft in the center and there are several large cracks on top, about 14 minutes. Cool the cookies on the baking sheets for 5 minutes, then use a wide metal spatula to transfer the cookies to a wire rack to cool completely.

The cookies can be stored in a tightly covered container at room temperature for up to 4 days.

makes 14 cookies • **cookie making** 15 minutes • **cookie baking** 350 degrees, two baking sheets for about 14 minutes each

chocolate caramel **pecan** clusters

Fast cars, fast food, fast cookies. No contest for me. I choose fast cookies, and these candy-like milk-chocolate-covered caramel and pecan cookies are about as fast as cookies get. The caramel sauce is made with brown sugar so it cooks in minutes, there is no baking at all, and making the chocolate coating is a matter of melting chocolate. As soon as the milk chocolate topping is set, the cookies are ready. The only hard part is waiting for the chocolate topping to firm up.

I boil the caramel sauce for 2 ¹/₂ minutes for a chewy result. Boiling the sauce for 2 minutes will result in a softer, stickier caramel, and 3 minutes will produce a firm caramel. This butter and brown sugar combination is a great method for producing a foolproof soft caramel that can also be used as a warm sundae sauce.

caramel sauce

- **3/4** cup (1 ¹/₂ sticks) unsalted butter, cut into pieces
- **1** cup packed light brown sugar
- **2** tablespoons honey
- **2 1/2** cups (about 10 ounces) pecan halves or large pieces

chocolate coating

- **6** ounces (generous 1 cup) milk chocolate chips or milk chocolate, chopped
- **1** tablespoon canola or corn oil

Grease a baking sheet lightly with oil and set aside. Set out a large spoon.

MAKE THE CARAMEL SAUCE. In a medium saucepan, cook the butter, brown sugar, and honey over medium heat, stirring often, until the butter and sugar melt. Increase the heat to medium-high and bring the mixture to a boil. Boil for exactly 2 ¹/₂ minutes, stirring constantly. Be sure to stir all around the edges of the pan to prevent burning. Remove from the heat and stir in the pecans, stirring to coat them with the caramel, then immediately use a large spoon to drop heaping tablespoons of the mixture 2 inches apart on the prepared baking sheet, making 12 mounds that measure about 3 by 2 ¹/₂ inches. Let cool completely. (As soon as the clusters are cool, they will slide easily off the oiled baking sheet.)

MAKE THE CHOCOLATE COATING. Put the milk chocolate and oil in a heatproof container or the top of a double boiler and place it over, but not touching, a saucepan of barely simmering water (or the bottom of the double boiler). Stir until the chocolate is melted and smooth. Remove from the water and let cool and thicken slightly, 15 to 20 minutes.

Spoon about 2 teaspoons of the chocolate coating over the top of each cookie (use all of the chocolate coating) so some chocolate drizzles down the sides.

The clusters should not be completely covered with chocolate. Let the cookie clusters sit at room temperature until the chocolate coating is firm, about 1 hour. Or, to speed the firming of the chocolate, refrigerate the cookies for about 20 minutes.

The cookies can be stored, covered and in a single layer in the refrigerator, for up to 3 days. Serve at room temperature. The cookies will become firm and brittle when cold but soften when brought back to room temperature.

choices

Make a dark chocolate coating rather than a milk chocolate one by melting 1 cup (6 ounces) semisweet chocolate chips with the oil.

makes 12 cookies • **cookie making** 20 minutes • **cookie baking** none

jumbo black bottom **coconut** macaroons

• •

These are the macaroons that ended my quest for thick mounds of moist-on-the-inside and crisp-on-the-outside coconut macaroons. Dipping the cookie bottoms in chocolate coating is a simple step that adds a professional look to the cookies. To produce a firm, shiny chocolate coating, the chocolate is melted with a bit of vegetable oil. Coconut macaroons can be served cold or at room temperature, but I prefer the dense, more chewy texture of cold macaroons.

cookies

one	7-ounce bag (2 $2/3$ cups) shredded sweetened coconut
$1/2$	cup sweetened condensed milk
$1/8$	teaspoon salt
1 $1/2$	teaspoons almond extract
$1/2$	teaspoon vanilla extract
1	large egg white
pinch	of cream of tartar
1	tablespoon sugar

chocolate coating

9	ounces semisweet chocolate, chopped
1	tablespoon canola or corn oil

Position a rack in the middle of the oven. Preheat the oven to 350 degrees F. Line a baking sheet with parchment paper and butter the paper.

MAKE THE COOKIES. In a large bowl, use a fork to stir the coconut, condensed milk, salt, almond extract, and vanilla together. Set aside.

In an impeccably clean medium bowl, use a whisk or a hand-held mixer on low speed to beat the egg white with the cream of tartar until they are foamy and the cream of tartar dissolves. Whisking vigorously or beating on medium-high speed, beat until soft peaks form. Whisk or beat in the sugar. Use a rubber spatula to fold half of the whipped egg white into the coconut mixture, then fold in the remaining white.

Using an ice cream scoop or measuring cup with a $1/4$-cup capacity, scoop mounds of the coconut batter onto the prepared baking sheet, spacing the macaroons 2 inches apart.

Bake until the bottoms of the cookies and the tips of the coconut shreds are light brown, about 17 minutes. Cool the cookies on the baking sheet for 5 minutes, then slide a metal spatula under the macaroons to loosen them from the parchment and transfer them to a wire rack to cool completely.

. . . . recipe continued next page

MAKE THE CHOCOLATE COATING. Put the chocolate and oil in a heatproof container or the top of a double boiler and place it over, but not touching, a saucepan of barely simmering water (or the bottom of the double boiler). Stir until the chocolate is melted and smooth. Remove from the water and let cool and thicken slightly, about 10 minutes.

Scrape the chocolate coating into a small bowl. Dip the bottom of each macaroon in the chocolate and place the cookies, chocolate bottoms up or on their sides, on a wire rack.(You will have some chocolate coating left over for another use or to pour over ice cream. It's easier to dip using a larger amount of coating.) Let the macaroons sit at room temperature until the chocolate coating is firm, about 1 hour. Or, to speed the firming of the chocolate, refrigerate the macaroons on the rack for about 15 minutes. Serve cold or at room temperature.

The cookies can be stored in a covered container in the refrigerator for up to 5 days.

makes 9 cookies • **cookie making** 25 minutes • **cookie baking** 350 degrees, for about 17 minutes

pineapple and macadamia **islands**

Take a trip to the tropics—with a cookie, that is. Loaded with dried pineapple and macadamia nuts, dependably available year–round, these cookies can whisk you away to a fantasy island at the drop of a spoonful of dough.

Slices or cubes of sweetened dried pineapple can be found in natural foods stores and often in the natural foods section of supermarkets. I use salted macadamia nuts, which are easier to find than unsalted, but I discard any salt that falls off the nuts when I chop them. Spoon, rather than scrape, the chopped nuts into the measuring cup so the salt remains on the cutting surface.

1 1/4	cups unbleached all-purpose flour
1	teaspoon baking soda
1/2	teaspoon salt
1/2	cup (1 stick) unsalted butter, melted
1	cup sugar
1	large egg
1	teaspoon vanilla extract
2	teaspoons rum, preferably dark
3/4	cup (about 3 3/4 ounces) macadamia nuts, coarsely chopped
1	cup sweetened dried pineapple (about 4 slices, or 5 ounces), cut into 1/4- to 1/2-inch pieces

Position a rack in the middle of the oven. Preheat the oven to 350 degrees. Line two baking sheets with parchment paper.

In a small bowl, stir the flour, baking soda, and salt together; set aside. In a large bowl, using a large spoon, stir the melted butter and sugar to blend them. The mixture will look grainy. Stir in the egg, vanilla, and rum until the mixture looks smooth and shiny. Stir in the flour mixture to incorporate it. Stir in the macadamia nuts and pineapple pieces.

Using an ice cream scoop or measuring cup with a 1/4-cup capacity, scoop mounds of the dough onto the prepared baking sheets, spacing the cookies 3 inches apart. Bake the cookies one sheet at a time until the tops are light golden, about 14 minutes. The cookies will puff up during baking, then flatten slightly just before they are done. Cool the cookies on the baking sheets for 5 minutes, then use a wide metal spatula to transfer them to a wire rack to cool completely.

The cookies can be stored in a tightly covered container at room temperature for up to 3 days.

makes 10 cookies · **cookie making** 15 minutes · **cookie baking** 350 degrees, two baking sheets for about 14 minutes each

morning glory **breakfast** cookies

No time for breakfast? Grab a couple of these carrot, fruit, and nut cookies and take breakfast with you. The dough for these soft cookies is sticky, so an ice cream scoop works best for forming the cookies. Although the ingredient list looks rather long, most of these are items that are likely to be on hand.

2 3/4	cups unbleached all-purpose flour
1	teaspoon baking powder
1/4	teaspoon salt
1	teaspoon ground cinnamon
3/4	cup (1 1/2 sticks) unsalted butter, at room temperature
1 3/4	cups granulated sugar
1	teaspoon finely grated orange zest
2	large eggs
2	teaspoons vanilla extract
1	cup finely grated or chopped peeled carrots (2 or 3 carrots)
3/4	cup grated peeled apple (1 apple)
1	cup raisins
1/2	cup shredded sweetened coconut
1	cup coarsely chopped walnuts

Powdered sugar for dusting
(optional)

Position a rack in the middle of the oven. Preheat the oven to 350 degrees F. Line two baking sheets with parchment paper.

Sift the flour, baking powder, salt, and cinnamon into a medium bowl and set aside. In a large bowl, using an electric mixer on medium speed, beat the butter, sugar, and orange zest until smoothly blended, about 1 minute. Stop the mixer and scrape the sides of the bowl as needed during mixing. Add the eggs and vanilla and mix until blended, about 1 minute. Mix in the carrots, apple, raisins, coconut, and walnuts. The batter will become quite liquid from the moist carrots and apples. On low speed, add the flour mixture, mixing just until incorporated. The dough will be soft and sticky.

Using an ice cream scoop, preferably, or measuring cup with a 1/4-cup capacity, scoop mounds of the dough onto the prepared baking sheets, spacing the cookies at least 2 1/2 inches apart. Bake the cookies one sheet at a time until the bottoms are browned, the tops are pale but firm, and a toothpick inserted in the center of a cookie comes out dry, about 20 minutes. Cool the cookies on the baking sheets for 5 minutes, then use a wide metal spatula to transfer the cookies to a wire rack to cool completely.

Dust the cooled cookies with powdered sugar, if desired. The cookies can be stored in a tightly covered container at room temperature for up to 4 days.

makes 20 cookies • **cookie making** 20 minutes • **cookie baking** 350 degrees, two baking sheets for about 20 minutes each

big city **black-and-whites**

These cookies are like the best part of a cupcake—the top with the frosting. The soft, moist cookies form slightly mounded tops during baking, and the baked cookies are turned flat bottom side up for glazing. One half of the bottom is spread with chocolate glaze, and the other half with white glaze. I used to buy black-and-whites when I spent summers in Brooklyn as a kid. I always searched the bakery shelf for the cookies with the thickest, shiniest glaze, so you can bet that I made sure my version has a generous coating of glaze. Although this cookie involves preparing two glazes, both are easy to make.

cookies

- 1 3/4 cups unbleached all-purpose flour
- 1/2 teaspoon baking powder
- 1/2 teaspoon baking soda
- 1/4 teaspoon salt
- 1/2 cup (1 stick) unsalted butter, at room temperature
- 3/4 cup sugar
- 1 teaspoon finely grated lemon zest
- 2 large eggs
- 1 teaspoon vanilla extract
- 1/4 teaspoon almond extract
- 1/2 cup buttermilk (any fat content is fine)

chocolate glaze

- 1/3 cup heavy (whipping) cream
- 4 tablespoons (1/2 stick) unsalted butter, cut into pieces
- 3 tablespoons light corn syrup
- 1 cup (6 ounces) chocolate chips or chopped semisweet chocolate

white glaze

- 2 cups powdered sugar
- 3 tablespoons, plus up to 2 teaspoons hot water if necessary
- 1 teaspoon corn syrup
- 1/4 teaspoon almond extract

Position a rack in the middle of the oven. Preheat the oven to 350 degrees F. Line a baking sheet with parchment paper and butter the paper.

MAKE THE COOKIES. In a medium bowl, stir the flour, baking powder, baking soda, and salt together; set aside. In a large bowl, using an electric mixer on medium speed, beat the butter, sugar, and lemon zest until smooth and slightly lightened in color, about 1 minute. Stop the mixer and scrape the sides of the bowl as needed during mixing. Beat in the eggs, vanilla, and almond extract until blended, about 1 minute. On low speed, mix in half of the flour mixture just to incorporate it. Mix in the buttermilk, blending completely. Mix in the remaining flour mixture.

recipe continued next page

• • • • • • • • • • • • • • • •

Using an ice cream scoop or measuring cup with a $^1/_4$-cup capacity, scoop mounds of the dough onto the prepared baking sheet, spacing the cookies at least 2 $^1/_2$ inches apart. Bake the cookies until the edges and bottoms are lightly browned and a toothpick inserted in the center comes out dry, about 14 minutes. Cool the cookies on the baking sheet for 5 minutes, then use a wide metal spatula to transfer them to a wire rack to cool completely.

MAKE THE CHOCOLATE GLAZE. In a medium saucepan, heat the cream, butter, and corn syrup over medium heat until the mixture is hot and the butter melts; do not let boil. Remove the pan from the heat and add the chocolate chips. Let the chocolate melt for about 30 seconds, then stir until all of the chocolate has melted and the glaze is smooth. Let the glaze cool until it thickens enough to cling to the cookies, about 30 minutes.

MAKE THE WHITE GLAZE. When ready to glaze the cookies, in a medium bowl, stir the powdered sugar, 3 tablespoons of the hot water, corn syrup, and almond extract together to make a thick, smooth, pourable glaze. If necessary, continue adding hot water by the teaspoon to reach the desired consistency.

Turn the cookies so the flat bottom sides are up. Spoon about 1 tablespoon of the white glaze on one side of what is now the top of a cookie and use the back of the spoon to spread the glaze evenly over half of the cookie. (If the glaze thickens as you work so it does not spread easily, add a few drops of water.) Repeat with the remaining cookies. Spoon a generous 1 tablespoon of chocolate glaze over the bare half of each cookie, spreading it evenly over that half of the cookie. Some glaze may drip over the sides, and that is fine. (You will have about 3 tablespoons chocolate glaze left for another use.) Refrigerate the cookies to firm the glaze.

Wrap each cookie in plastic wrap and refrigerate. Serve cold or at room temperature. The cookies can be stored in the refrigerator for up to 3 days.

choices

Substitute 1 teaspoon finely grated orange zest for the lemon zest.

makes 9 cookies • **cookie making** 30 minutes • **cookie baking** 350 degrees, for about 14 minutes

colossal**crisp**cookies

From cookie brittle to buttery shortbread to peanut-covered cookie slabs, crisp cookies run the gamut. A lot goes into making a cookie crisp—ingredients and their proportions, baking times, and such additions as nuts, toasted coconut, melted sugar, or toffee. Some of these cookies are crisp all the way through, others have the contrast of a soft center or soft pieces of fruit. Vanilla Butter Rounds, for example, are completely crisp, while Cinnamon Sugar Snickerdoodles have a crunchy sugar topping and crisp edges but a slightly chewy center.

Cookie ingredients act in different ways to make cookies crisp. Flour absorbs moisture, so more flour can make cookies crisper, but too much flour can make them dry. The trick is to add just enough flour to make crisp, tender cookies, not "cookie rocks." Sugar also contributes to a crisp texture, with white sugar producing a crisper result than the slightly moister brown sugar. Some of these cookies use a combination of sugars, white for crispness and brown for its flavor. Vegetable shortening makes a crisper cookie than butter. A combination of the two yields a cookie that has both crispness and buttery flavor. I have also discovered that using melted butter in chocolate chip–type doughs produces a crisp result.

Baking is in part a drying-out process, so the longer a cookie bakes, the crisper it becomes. Of course you must be careful not to bake cookies too long or to burn them. Biscotti are a familiar example. They are actually baked twice, and for a long time, but at a low temperature.

Drop, spread, and roll are not firefighting instructions here but methods for forming these cookies. Some crisp cookies are made by the drop method. The doughs in two of these cookie recipes are spread into large irregular slabs, baked, and broken into cookie bark or cookie brittle when cool. The doughs for Big-Hearted Butter Shortbread and Celebration Sugar Cookies are rolled out and cut into various shapes. The shapes are limited only by the cookie cutters you have and your imagination. The doughs for other of these cookies are rolled into balls, and sometimes flattened into disks. Another method used here is to form the dough into logs or slabs that are sliced and baked. This method produces a lot of cookies quickly. And the dough logs can be frozen, ready to defrost, slice, and bake whenever they are needed.

chocolate chunk **mountains**

Some uncles bring family mementos to weddings. My Uncle Howie brought these cookies to my son's wedding, with an urgent request to figure out how to duplicate them. One taste of these walnut and chocolate–all–the–way–through cookie mounds convinced me that my uncle had brought something truly special.

When the cookies are still warm, the insides are very soft and the chocolate chunks melted. When cooled for at least four hours, the cookies and the chocolate chunks are firm yet at the same time pleasingly soft against the contrasting crunch of the walnuts. Feel free to enjoy them at both stages—I do.

Semisweet chocolate chunks can be found with the chocolate chips in the baking section of supermarkets. Each bag weighs 11 1/2 ounces and holds about 2 cups of chocolate chunks. Or you can chop up bars of semisweet chocolate into 1/4- to 1/2-inch chunks. Baking these cookies for exactly 10 minutes produces cookies that are firm on the outside and soft inside.

3 ounces unsweetened chocolate, chopped

2 3/4 cups unbleached all-purpose flour

2 teaspoons cream of tartar

1 teaspoon baking soda

1/4 teaspoon salt

1/2 cup (1 stick) unsalted butter, at room temperature

1/2 cup vegetable shortening, such as Crisco

1 cup granulated sugar

1/2 cup packed light brown sugar

2 large eggs

2 teaspoons vanilla extract

1 teaspoon instant coffee granules, dissolved in **2** teaspoons water

1 cup (about 4 ounces) walnuts, coarsely chopped

3 cups (about 17 ounces) semisweet chocolate chunks or chopped semisweet chocolate

Position a rack in the middle of the oven. Preheat the oven to 350 degrees F. Line two baking sheets with parchment paper.

Put the unsweetened chocolate in a heatproof container or the top of a double boiler and place it over, but not touching, a saucepan of barely simmering water (or the bottom of the double boiler). Stir the chocolate until it is melted and smooth. Remove from the water and set aside to cool slightly.

Sift the flour, cream of tartar, baking soda, and salt into a medium bowl and set aside. In a large bowl, using an electric mixer on low speed, beat the butter, vegetable shortening, granulated sugar, and brown sugar until well blended and smooth, about 1 minute. Stop the mixer and scrape the sides of the bowl as needed during mixing. Mix in the melted chocolate. Mix in the eggs, vanilla, and dissolved coffee until smoothly blended, about 1 minute. Add the flour mixture, mixing just until it is incorporated. Mix in the nuts and chocolate chunks.

Using an ice cream scoop or measuring cup with a 1/4-cup capacity, scoop out portions of dough, roll each one between the palms of your hands into a smooth ball, and place on the prepared baking sheets, spacing the cookies 2 inches apart.

Bake the cookies one sheet at a time for 10 minutes. The outsides of the cookies will change from shiny to dull and the tops should feel firm but the interior will still be quite soft; the cookies will firm up as they cool.

Cool the cookies for 15 minutes on the baking sheets, then use a wide metal spatula to transfer them to a wire rack to cool thoroughly. It will take at least 4 hours for the chocolate to firm up. If leaving them to cool overnight, put the cookies on a plate and cover them. They are especially good served the day after baking.

The cookies can be stored in a tightly covered container at room temperature for up to 4 days.

makes 23 cookies • **cookie making** 20 minutes • **cookie baking** 350 degrees, two baking sheets for about 10 minutes each

chocolate chip **whoppers**

· ·

When I turned in a final recipe list for this book, my editor, Bill LeBlond, said that the list looked just right except that he missed a crisp chocolate chip cookie. It was a broad hint and a good idea. These are for Bill and all of the fans of crisp-all-the-way-through chocolate chip cookies, including me.

Two ingredients, or actually the lack of one, contribute to the crisp texture: the butter is melted rather than softened and there is no egg in the dough.

2 cups unbleached all-purpose flour
1 teaspoon baking soda
3/4 teaspoon salt
1 cup (2 sticks) unsalted butter, melted and cooled slightly
3/4 cup granulated sugar
3/4 cup packed light brown sugar
1 teaspoon vanilla extract
3 tablespoons water
2 cups (12 ounces) semisweet chocolate chips
1 cup (about 4 ounces) walnuts or pecans, coarsely chopped (optional)

Position a rack in the middle of the oven. Preheat the oven to 350 degrees F. Line two baking sheets with parchment paper.

Sift the flour, baking soda, and salt into a medium bowl and set aside. In a large bowl, using an electric mixer on low speed, mix the melted butter, granulated sugar, brown sugar, and vanilla until smooth, about 30 seconds. Stop the mixer and scrape the sides of the bowl as needed during mixing. Add the flour mixture, mixing just until it is incorporated. The dough will look crumbly. Mix in the water. The dough will become soft and smooth. Stir in the chocolate chips and nuts, if desired.

Using an ice cream scoop or measuring cup with a $^1/_4$-cup capacity, scoop mounds of the dough onto the prepared baking sheets, spacing the cookies at least 3 inches apart. Gently press the cookies to flatten them slightly, to about $^3/_4$ inch thick.

Bake the cookies one sheet at a time until the tops are evenly lightly browned and have a few cracks, about 17 minutes. Cool the cookies for 5 minutes on the baking sheets, then use a wide metal spatula to transfer them to a wire rack to cool thoroughly.

The cookies can be stored in a tightly covered container at room temperature for up to 4 days.

makes 15 cookies · **cookie making** 10 minutes · **cookie baking** 350 degrees, two baking sheets for about 17 minutes each

chocolate **peppermint crunch** cookie bark

● ●

Part cookie, part candy, these are shards of crisp dark chocolate chip cookie topped with crushed peppermint candy.
The chocolate dough is baked as two big cookie slabs, then a heavy scattering of chocolate chips is allowed to melt
on top of the warm cookies and the candy pieces are sprinkled over the chocolate. The melted chocolate anchors the
pieces so they will not fall off when the cooled cookie is snapped into irregular pieces. Instead of peppermint candy,
the bark could also be topped with crushed toffee or chopped white chocolate. I do not line the baking sheets with
parchment paper for this recipe, as the paper would slide around when the dough was spread onto the baking sheets.

cookie base

1 **1/2**	cups unbleached all-purpose flour
3/4	teaspoon baking soda
1/2	teaspoon salt
1/2	cup unsweetened Dutch-process cocoa powder
1	cup (2 sticks) unsalted butter, melted and cooled slightly
3/4	cup granulated sugar
1/2	cup packed light brown sugar
2	tablespoons water
2	teaspoons vanilla extract
1 **1/2**	cups (9 ounces) semisweet chocolate chips

topping

1 **1/2**	cups (9 ounces) semisweet chocolate chips
3/4	cup (about 5 ounces) crushed peppermint candy (crush with a rolling pin into small pieces)

Position a rack in the middle of the oven. Preheat the oven to 350 degrees F. Have ready two baking sheets.

PREPARE THE COOKIE BASE. In a medium bowl, stir the flour, baking soda, and salt together. Sift the cocoa powder onto the flour mixture and set aside.

In a large bowl, using an electric mixer on low speed, mix the melted butter, granulated sugar, brown sugar, water, and vanilla until smooth, about 30 seconds. Stop the mixer and scrape the sides of the bowl as needed during mixing. Add the flour mixture, mixing just until the flour is incorporated. Stir in the chocolate chips.

Leaving a 3-inch border empty on all sides, use a thin metal spatula to spread half of the dough on one baking sheet into a rough rectangle that measures about 11 by 8 inches and is about $1/4$ inch thick. Use the palms of your hands to help pat it into an even layer. Repeat with the remaining cookie dough on the second baking sheet.

recipe continued next page

● ● ● ● ● ● ● ● ● ● ● ● ● ● ● ● ●

Bake one baking sheet at a time until the top looks dull, not shiny, and feels evenly firm at the edges and center, about 14 minutes. As soon as each baking sheet comes out of the oven, sprinkle $3/4$ cup of the chocolate chips over the cookie slab. Let the chocolate chips sit for 5 minutes to soften and melt, then use a small metal spatula to spread the melted chocolate over the cookie, covering most of the cookie. While the chocolate is still warm, sprinkle half the peppermint candy evenly over the slab.

Let the cookie bark cool on the baking sheets on a wire rack until the chocolate topping is firm, about 2 hours. Or, to speed the cooling, cool the cookies on the baking sheets for about 30 minutes, then refrigerate them, still on the baking sheets, just until the chocolate topping firms, then remove from the refrigerator. The cookie bark will become crisp as it cools.

Break each cookie slab into about twelve 5- to 6-inch-long irregular pieces. The cookies can be stored layered between sheets of wax paper in a tightly covered container at room temperature for up to 5 days.

makes about twenty-four 5- to 6-inch-long irregularly shaped cookies ● **cookie making** 25 minutes
cookie baking 350 degrees, two baking sheets for about 14 minutes each

toffee crunch cookie brittle

There is no doubt about it, this cookie is total crunch. It has crushed toffee, big pieces of walnuts, and a crisp brown sugar cookie base to hold it all together. To avoid pieces of toffee skidding around the kitchen, leave the candy bars in their wrappers when you crush them with a hammer or meat pounder.

1 1/2 cups unbleached all-purpose flour
1/2 teaspoon baking soda
1/2 teaspoon salt
3/4 cup (1 1/2 sticks) unsalted butter, melted and cooled slightly
1/2 cup granulated sugar
1/3 cup packed light brown sugar
1 teaspoon vanilla extract
1 1/2 cups (about 7 ounces) crushed chocolate-covered toffee, such as Heath Bars or Skor
1 cup (about 4 ounces) walnuts, broken into large pieces

Position a rack in the middle of the oven. Preheat the oven to 350 degrees F. Line a baking sheet with parchment paper.

In a medium bowl, stir the flour, baking soda, and salt together; set aside. In a large bowl, whisk the melted butter, granulated sugar, brown sugar, and vanilla until smooth, about 30 seconds. Use a large spoon to stir in the flour mixture. The dough should look smooth. Stir in the crushed toffee and walnuts. The dough will look crumbly.

Leaving a 1- to 1 $1/2$-inch border empty on all sides, spoon the dough onto the prepared baking sheet. Press the dough into a rectangle that measures about 13 by 9 inches and is about $1/2$ inch thick, then use the palms of your hands to pat it into an even layer.

Bake until the top feels firm and looks dark golden and the edges look light brown, about 19 minutes. Let the cookie brittle cool on the baking sheet for 10 minutes, then use a large metal spatula to slide the cookie onto a wire rack to cool. (Don't worry if the cookie breaks; it will be broken into pieces when cool.) The cookie will become crisp as it cools.

Break the cooled cookie into 4- to 5-inch pieces. The cookies can be stored in a tightly covered container at room temperature for up to 4 days.

makes about twelve 4- to 5-inch-long irregularly shaped cookies • **cookie making** 15 minutes
cookie baking 350 degrees for about 19 minutes

vanilla **butter** rounds

Cake flour is the secret to the especially tender texture of these cookies, with lots of butter and a generous measure of vanilla working together to create the rich taste. Let the bottoms and edges of these cookies brown lightly to give the cookies a pleasing browned butter flavor. Look for boxes of cake flour (not self-rising) in the supermarket.

2 3/4 cups cake flour
1/2 teaspoon baking powder
1/4 teaspoon salt
1 1/2 cups (3 sticks) unsalted butter, at room temperature
1 cup sugar
3 large egg yolks
2 teaspoons vanilla extract
1/4 teaspoon almond extract
18 whole unblanched (with skins) almonds or pecan or walnut halves (optional)

Sift the cake flour, baking powder, and salt into a medium bowl and set aside. In a large bowl, using an electric mixer on medium speed, beat the butter and sugar until lightened in color and fluffy, about 2 minutes. Stop the mixer and scrape the sides of the bowl as needed during mixing. Mix in the egg yolks, vanilla, and almond extract until smoothly blended, about 1 minute. On low speed, add the flour mixture, mixing just until it is incorporated. The dough will be soft and sticky. Cover the bowl with plastic wrap and refrigerate until the dough is cold and firm enough to roll into balls with your hands without sticking, about 1 hour.

Position a rack in the middle of the oven. Preheat the oven to 325 degrees F. Line two baking sheets with parchment paper.

Using an ice cream scoop or measuring cup with a $^1/_4$-cup capacity, scoop out mounds of dough. Roll each mound between the palms of your hands into a smooth ball, flatten it into a 3-inch circle, and place the cookies 2 inches apart on the prepared baking sheets. Press a nut into the center of each cookie, if desired.

Bake the cookies one sheet at a time until the edges are light brown, about 22 minutes. Cool the cookies for 5 minutes on the baking sheets, then use a wide metal spatula to transfer the cookies to a wire rack to cool completely.

The cookies can be stored in a tightly covered container at room temperature for up to 5 days.

makes 18 cookies • **cookie making** 20 minutes, plus chilling time • **cookie baking** 325 degrees, two baking sheets for about 22 minutes each

peanut butter cup cookies

Ice cream shops often make ice cream even better by adding candy and cookie mix–ins. Along the lines of that good idea, these cookies have peanut butter cup pieces mixed into a peanut butter dough.

1 cup unbleached all-purpose flour
1/2 teaspoon baking soda
1/8 teaspoon salt
1/4 cup (1/2 stick) unsalted butter, at room temperature
1/4 cup (4 tablespoons) vegetable shortening, such as Crisco
3/4 cup smooth peanut butter, at room temperature
1/2 cup packed light brown sugar
1/3 cup granulated sugar
1 large egg
1 teaspoon vanilla extract
2 cups (about 9 1/2 ounces) peanut butter cups, cut into 1/2- to 3/4-inch pieces

Position a rack in the middle of the oven. Preheat the oven to 325 degrees F. Line two baking sheets with parchment paper.

Sift the flour, baking soda, and salt into a medium bowl and set aside. In a large bowl, using an electric mixer on medium speed, beat the butter, vegetable shortening, peanut butter, brown sugar, and granulated sugar until smoothly blended and the color has lightened slightly, about 1 minute. Stop the mixer and scrape the sides of the bowl as needed during mixing. Mix in the egg and vanilla, about 1 minute. On low speed, add the flour mixture, mixing just until it is incorporated. The dough will be soft and smooth. Use a large spoon to mix in the peanut butter cup pieces.

Drop heaping tablespoons (about 3 level tablespoons each) of dough onto the prepared baking sheets, spacing them 3 inches apart. Bake the cookies one sheet at a time until the tops feel firm and have several small cracks, about 18 minutes. Cool the cookies for 5 minutes on the baking sheets, then use a wide metal spatula to transfer them to a wire rack to cool thoroughly.

The cookies can be stored in a tightly covered container at room temperature for up to 4 days.

makes 20 cookies · **cookie making** 20 minutes · **cookie baking** 325 degrees, two baking sheets for about 18 minutes each

cherry, cashew, and **white chocolate chunk** saucers

* *

Many cookies benefit from the addition of fruit, nuts, or chocolate, but these cookies go all out: they include all three. The recipe calls for chunks of white chocolate, but white chocolate chips can be substituted. Check to see that the package says white chocolate chips rather than white baking chips—then you'll know you are getting real white chocolate that contains cocoa butter.

1 1/4 cups unbleached all-purpose flour
1/2 teaspoon baking soda
1/4 teaspoon salt
3/4 cup (1 1/2 sticks) unsalted butter, at room temperature
1/2 cup granulated sugar
1/2 cup packed light brown sugar
1 large egg
1 tablespoon fresh lemon juice
1 teaspoon vanilla extract
3/4 teaspoon almond extract
3/4 cup (about 4 ounces) dried cherries
1 cup (5 ounces) unsalted roasted cashew halves
4 ounces white chocolate, chopped into 1/4- to 1/2-inch pieces

Position a rack in the middle of the oven. Preheat the oven to 350 degrees F. Line two baking sheets with parchment paper.

Sift the flour, baking soda, and salt into a medium bowl and set aside. In a large bowl, using an electric mixer on medium speed, beat the butter, granulated sugar, and brown sugar until smoothly blended, about 1 minute. Stop the mixer and scrape the sides of the bowl as needed during mixing. Mix in the egg, lemon juice, vanilla, and almond extract until blended, about 1 minute. The mixture may look curdled. On low speed, add the flour mixture, mixing just until it is incorporated and the dough looks smooth. Mix in the cherries, cashews, and white chocolate.

Using an ice cream scoop or measuring cup with a 1/4-cup capacity, scoop mounds of the dough onto the prepared baking sheets, spacing the cookies 3 inches apart. Bake the cookies one sheet at a time until the edges are light brown, but the centers are light golden, about 14 minutes. Cool the cookies for 5 minutes on the baking sheets, then use a wide metal spatula to transfer the cookies to a wire rack to cool completely.

The cookies can be stored in a tightly covered container at room temperature for up to 4 days.

makes 16 cookies · **cookie making** 15 minutes · **cookie baking** 350 degrees, two baking sheets for about 14 minutes each

orange-pecan **brown sugar** cookies

"Gosh, does this house smell good," I always remark when I bake these cookies. That is what happens when butter and brown sugar bake together. With a baking scent that good, you can imagine the taste these cookies have. Because cornstarch is used in place of some of the flour, they have an especially tender texture.

2 1/2	cups unbleached all-purpose flour
1/4	cup cornstarch
1/2	teaspoon salt
1 1/2	cups (3 sticks) unsalted butter, at room temperature
1 1/2	cups packed dark brown sugar
4	teaspoons finely grated orange zest
2	teaspoons vanilla extract
2 1/2	cups (about 10 ounces) finely chopped pecans

Powdered sugar for dusting (optional)

Position a rack in the middle of the oven. Preheat the oven to 350 degrees F. Line two baking sheets with parchment paper.

Sift the flour, cornstarch, and salt into a medium bowl and set aside. In a large bowl, using an electric mixer on medium speed, beat the butter and brown sugar until smoothly blended, about 1 minute. Stop the mixer and scrape the sides of the bowl as needed during mixing. Mix in the orange zest, vanilla, and 1 1/2 cups of the pecans until blended, about 1 minute. On low speed, add the flour mixture, mixing just until it is completely incorporated.

Using an ice cream scoop or measuring cup with a 1/4-cup capacity, scoop out portions of dough. Roll each one between the palms of your hands into a smooth ball, flatten it into a 3 1/2- inch circle, and place the cookies 2 inches apart on the baking sheets. Sprinkle the remaining pecans over the centers of the cookies, pressing them gently into the dough.

Bake one sheet at a time until the tops feel firm when gently touched and the bottoms are lightly browned, about 20 minutes (the color change during baking is subtle; the unbaked dough is light brown and the baked cookie tops and bottoms will be a medium brown). The cookies will spread quite a bit and be about 4 1/2 inches in diameter after baking. Cool the cookies for 10 minutes on the baking sheets, then use a wide metal spatula to transfer them to a wire rack to cool thoroughly. The cookies will become crisp as they cool.

Dust the cookies lightly with powdered sugar, if desired. The cookies can be stored in a tightly covered container at room temperature for up to 5 days.

makes 16 cookies • **cookie making** 20 minutes • **cookie baking** 350 degrees, two baking sheets for about 20 minutes each

chocolate **cherry** oatmeal cookies

Soft milk chocolate chips and chewy dried cherries add another dimension to crisp chocolate oatmeal cookies.
Reliably sweet and always in season, dried cherries make these a good any-season fruit choice. Or mix-and-match
white or dark chocolate chips and/or dried cranberries or chopped dried apricots for other combinations.

1 3/4 cups unbleached all-purpose flour
1/4 cup unsweetened Dutch-process cocoa powder
1 teaspoon baking powder
1 teaspoon baking soda
1/2 teaspoon salt
1/2 teaspoon ground cinnamon
1 cup (2 sticks) unsalted butter, at room temperature
1 cup granulated sugar
1 cup packed light brown sugar
2 large eggs
1 teaspoon vanilla extract
1 teaspoon almond extract
2 1/2 cups oatmeal (not quick-cooking)
1 cup (about 5 ounces) dried cherries
2 cups (11 1/2 ounces) milk chocolate chips

Position a rack in the middle of the oven. Preheat the oven to 325 degrees F. Line two baking sheets with parchment paper.

Sift the flour, cocoa powder, baking powder, baking soda, salt, and cinnamon into a medium bowl and set aside. In a large bowl, using an electric mixer on medium speed, beat the butter, granulated sugar, and brown sugar until smoothly blended, about 1 minute. Stop the mixer and scrape the sides of the bowl as needed during mixing. Add the eggs, vanilla, and almond extract and mix until blended, about 1 minute. The mixture may look curdled. On low speed, add the flour mixture and oatmeal, mixing just until the flour is incorporated and the dough looks smooth again. Mix in the dried cherries and chocolate chips.

Using an ice cream scoop or measuring cup with a $^1/_4$-cup capacity, scoop mounds of the dough onto the prepared baking sheets, spacing the cookies at least 2 $^1/_2$ inches apart. Bake the cookies one sheet at a time until the tops feel firm and look dull rather than shiny, about 22 minutes. Cool the cookies on the baking sheets for 5 minutes, then use a wide metal spatula to transfer them to a wire rack to cool completely.

The cookies can be stored in a tightly covered container at room temperature for up to 4 days.

makes 23 cookies · **cookie making** 15 minutes · **cookie baking** 325 degrees, two baking sheets for about 22 minutes each

top-heavy **heavenly** hash

In plain view, right on top—that is where the heap of marshmallows, walnuts, and chocolate chips sits on these crisp chocolate cookies. If I had the good luck to see a cookie like this one in a bakery case, I'd buy them all.

1 1/3 cups (8 ounces) semisweet chocolate chips

1 1/3 cups (about 5 1/2 ounces) walnuts, coarsely chopped

1 cup unbleached all-purpose flour

1/4 cup unsweetened Dutch-process cocoa powder

1 teaspoon baking soda

1/2 teaspoon salt

1/2 cup (1 stick) unsalted butter, melted

1 cup sugar

1 large egg

1 teaspoon vanilla extract

1 3/4 cups miniature marshmallows

Position a rack in the middle of the oven. Preheat the oven to 325 degrees. Line two baking sheets with parchment paper.

In a medium bowl, stir the chocolate chips and walnuts together; set aside. Sift the flour, cocoa powder, baking soda, and salt into a small bowl and set aside. In a large bowl, using a large spoon, stir the melted butter and sugar to blend them. The mixture will look grainy. Stir in the egg and vanilla until the mixture looks smooth and shiny. Stir in the flour mixture to incorporate it.

Drop heaping tablespoons (about 3 level tablespoons each) of dough onto the prepared baking sheets, spacing them 4 inches apart. Bake one sheet of the cookies until the tops feel firm, about 14 minutes. The cookies will puff up during baking, then flatten.

Remove the hot cookies from the oven and, leaving a 1/2-inch plain edge all around, scatter about 12 marshmallows over each cookie. Sprinkle 2 tablespoons of the walnut–chocolate chip mixture over the marshmallows. Return the cookies to the oven, immediately turn off the oven, and leave the cookies in the oven for 5 minutes. Remove the cookies. The marshmallows will be soft and the chocolate chips will be melted but hold their shape. Cool the cookies for 10 minutes on the baking sheet, then use a wide metal spatula to transfer the cookies to a wire rack to cool thoroughly. Preheat the oven again and bake and top the second sheet of cookies.

The cookies can be stored in a tightly covered container at room temperature for up to 3 days.

makes 14 cookies · **cookie making** 15 minutes · **cookie baking** 325 degrees, two baking sheets for about 14 minutes each

cinnamon sugar **snickerdoodles**

Southerners, Midwesterners, New Englanders, and the Pennsylvania Dutch have all claimed to be the originators of these cookies. I'm going to give the credit for these old-fashioned cookies to Melissa Carlin's Ohio grandmother. Melissa, a friend of my daughter's, shared her family recipe for these simple vanilla cookies coated with cinnamon sugar. The leavening for the cookies is a combination of cream of tartar and baking soda, which was an early version of baking powder, and it signals the tried-and-true status of this recipe.

2 ³/₄ cups unbleached all-purpose flour
2 teaspoons cream of tartar
1 teaspoon baking soda
¹/₄ teaspoon salt
1 ³/₄ cups sugar
1 tablespoon ground cinnamon
¹/₂ cup (1 stick) unsalted butter, at room temperature
¹/₂ cup (8 tablespoons) vegetable shortening, such as Crisco
2 large eggs
1 teaspoon vanilla extract
¹/₂ teaspoon almond extract

Position a rack in the middle of the oven. Preheat the oven to 350 degrees F. Line two baking sheets with parchment paper.

Sift the flour, cream of tartar, baking soda, and salt into a medium bowl and set aside. In a small bowl, stir together ¹/₄ cup of the sugar and the cinnamon; set aside. In a large bowl, using an electric mixer on medium speed, beat the butter, vegetable shortening, and the remaining 1 ¹/₂ cups sugar until smooth and fluffy, about 1 minute. Stop the mixer and scrape the sides of the bowl as needed during mixing. Add the eggs, vanilla, and almond extract and mix until blended, about 1 minute. On low speed, add the flour mixture, mixing just until it is incorporated. The dough will be soft and smooth.

Using an ice cream scoop or measuring cup with a ¹/₄-cup capacity, scoop out portions of dough. Roll each one between the palms of your hands into a smooth ball, roll each ball in the cinnamon-sugar mixture to coat it evenly, and place the cookies 3 inches apart on the prepared baking sheets.

Bake the cookies one sheet at a time just until the bottoms and edges are golden, about 18 minutes. The centers of the cookies should feel firm on top and soft underneath—this indicates that the cookies will have the desired soft, slightly chewy center. Cool the cookies for 5 minutes on the baking sheets, then use a wide metal spatula to transfer them to a wire rack to cool thoroughly.

The cookies can be stored in a tightly covered container at room temperature for up to 3 days.

makes 18 cookies · **cookie making** 15 minutes · **cookie baking** 350 degrees, two baking sheets for about 18 minutes each

super **s'more** crisps

A nice thing happened on the way to figuring out this cookie version of the popular graham cracker, milk chocolate, and marshmallow s'mores combination. During baking, many of the marshmallows in the graham cracker crumb batter melt, the sugar in the marshmallows caramelizes, and the result is cookies with crisp bits of caramelized sugar throughout. You don't have to do anything to make it happen—baking does it automatically.

3/4 cup (1 1/2 sticks) unsalted butter, at room temperature
1/2 cup sugar
1 large egg
1 teaspoon vanilla extract
3 cups graham cracker crumbs
1/4 cup unbleached all-purpose flour
1/4 teaspoon salt
1 1/2 cups (about 8 1/2 ounces) milk chocolate chips
1 1/2 cups miniature marshmallows

chocolate coating (page 46)

Position a rack in the middle of the oven. Preheat the oven to 325 degrees F. Line two baking sheets with parchment paper.

MAKE THE COOKIES. In a large bowl, using an electric mixer on medium speed, beat the butter and sugar until smoothly blended, about 1 minute. Stop the mixer and scrape the sides of the bowl as needed during mixing. Add the egg and vanilla, mixing until blended, about 1 minute. On low speed, mix in the graham cracker crumbs, flour, and salt until a soft dough forms that comes away from the sides of the bowl. Mix in the chocolate chips and marshmallows.

Using an ice cream scoop or a measuring cup with a $1/4$-cup capacity, scoop portions of dough onto the prepared baking sheets, placing them 4 inches apart. Flatten each cookie slightly, to about $3/4$ inch thick.

Bake one sheet at a time until the tops feel firm and the marshmallows near the edges of the cookies have melted and become clear and caramelized, about 15 minutes. (Some of the marshmallows in the center will remain white.) Cool the cookies for 5 minutes on the baking sheets, then use a wide metal spatula to transfer them to a wire rack to cool.

Use a small spoon to drizzle the chocolate coating over the cooled cookies. Leave the cookies at room temperature until the chocolate is firm, about 1 hour. Or refrigerate the cookies for about 15 minutes.

The cookies can be individually wrapped in plastic wrap and stored at room temperature for up to 2 days.

makes 15 cookies · **cookie making** 20 minutes · **cookie baking** 325 degrees, two baking sheets for about 15 minutes each

celebration sugar cookies

● ●

Here are my requirements for an all-purpose dough for making great cut-out cookies:

1. A dough that is easy to mix.

2. A dough that rolls out easily, is not fussy about being rolled out several times, and does not mind if little hands squish and press it a bit.

3. A dough that holds the shape of the cut-out design when baked.

4. A dough that produces a cookie that remains in good condition for a week or more and can successfully travel to faraway friends and family.

Here is that cookie dough.

2 3/4	cups unbleached all-purpose flour
1/2	cup cornstarch
1	teaspoon baking powder
1/4	teaspoon salt
3/4	cup (1 1/2 sticks) unsalted butter, at room temperature
1/2	cup (8 tablespoons) vegetable shortening, such as Crisco
1	cup sugar
1	large egg
2	teaspoons vanilla extract
1/2	teaspoon almond extract

In a medium bowl, stir the flour, cornstarch, baking powder, and salt together; set aside. In a large bowl, using an electric mixer on medium speed, beat the butter, vegetable shortening, and sugar until smooth and slightly lightened in color, about 1 minute. Stop the mixer and scrape the sides of the bowl as needed during mixing. Add the egg, vanilla, and almond extract and mix until blended, about 1 minute. On low speed, add the flour mixture, mixing just to incorporate it. The dough will be soft and smooth.

Divide the dough in half and form it into 2 smooth disks about 6 inches in diameter. Wrap the disks in plastic wrap and refrigerate until firm enough to roll without sticking but not so hard that it is difficult to roll out, about 1 hour.

Position a rack in the middle of the oven. Preheat the oven to 350 degrees F. Line two baking sheets with parchment paper.

Lightly flour the rolling surface and rolling pin. Unwrap one piece of dough and roll it out to about a 12-inch circle that is $3/16$ inch thick. Using a 3 $1/2$- to 5-inch-long cookie cutter, cut out cookies. Place the cookie cutter carefully so you can cut out as many cookies as possible from each rolling. Use a thin metal

. . . . *recipe continued next page*

• •

spatula to transfer the cookies to the prepared baking sheets, placing them about 1 inch apart. Gather together the dough scraps and set aside. Unwrap the second piece of dough and repeat the rolling and cutting process.

Gather together all of the dough scraps, forming a smooth disk, and roll and cut out the dough. If there is still quite a bit of dough remaining, gather the scraps together and roll and cut the dough once again.

Bake one sheet at a time until the edges and bottoms of the cookies are lightly browned, about 14 minutes. Cool the cookies on the baking sheets for 5 minutes, then use a wide metal spatula to transfer them to a wire rack to cool completely.

The cookies can be layered between sheets of wax paper in a tightly covered container and stored at room temperature for up to 1 week.

NOTE: To make snowmen, cut out about a 3-inch circle for the body and a 2-inch circle for the head. Slightly overlap the 2 circles for each snowman on the baking sheets and press them together. Decorate with the Powdered Sugar Frosting (page 78).

choices and decorations

The basic dough can be flavored with 1 teaspoon finely grated orange, lemon, or lime zest, 2 tablespoons finely chopped candied ginger, or 1 1/2 teaspoons ground cinnamon. The ingredients can be doubled to make a larger batch of cookies.

Colored sugars or nonpareils can be sprinkled on the cookies before baking. Or the cookies can be glazed when warm with Powdered Sugar Glaze (page 81), or the cooled cookies can be frosted with Powdered Sugar Frosting and decorated with colored sprinkles or non-pareils. About 2 tablespoons colored sugar, sprinkles, or nonpareils will decorate 24 cookies. The cookies can also be half-dipped in melted chocolate, or melted chocolate can be drizzled over them.

makes about 24 large cookies (smaller cookie cutters produce more cookies)

cookie making 30 minutes (including decorating) plus chilling time • **cookie baking** 350 degrees, two baking sheets for about 14 minutes each

gingerbread **giants**

As soon as the first cool breeze blows in, it's time for us to make these huge gingerbread people. Long ago we decided that these crisp spice cookies taste too good and are too much fun to make to wait for the holidays—plus, my husband, Jeff, is always in the mood for gingerbread cookies.

Rolling the scraps more than three times toughens the gingerbread, so position the cookie cutter carefully to make as many cookies as possible from each rolling. I use raisins for buttons and facial features and a simple powdered sugar glaze to make squiggles for hair, zigzags for trim, and dots for little details. It looks good no matter what you do.

cookies

3 3/4	cups unbleached all-purpose flour
1	teaspoon baking powder
1/2	teaspoon baking soda
1	tablespoon plus **1** teaspoon ground ginger
1 1/2	teaspoons ground cinnamon
1/2	teaspoon ground nutmeg
1/2	teaspoon ground cloves
1/2	cup (1 stick) unsalted butter, cut into pieces
3/4	cup packed light brown sugar
1/3	cup unsulphured molasses
2	large eggs

Raisins for decorating

powdered sugar frosting

1	cup powdered sugar
2	tablespoons heavy whipping cream, plus up to **2** teaspoons if needed

MAKE THE COOKIES. Sift the flour, baking powder, baking soda, ginger, cinnamon, nutmeg, and cloves into a large bowl and set aside. In a medium saucepan, heat the butter, brown sugar, and molasses over low heat, stirring often, until the butter and sugar melt. Increase the heat to medium-high and bring to a boil. Immediately remove the saucepan from the heat, and let cool for 10 to 15 minutes.

Position a rack in the middle of the oven. Preheat the oven to 325 degrees F. Line two baking sheets with parchment paper.

In a medium bowl, whisk the eggs to blend the yolks and whites. Whisking constantly, slowly pour the slightly cooled molasses mixture over the eggs. On low speed, with an electric mixer, pour the liquid mixture into the flour mixture, mixing until it is incorporated and the dough holds together in large clumps and comes cleanly away from the sides of the bowl.

Divide the dough in half and form it into 2 rough rectangles about 6 inches long. Wrap 1 piece of dough in plastic wrap and set aside. Lightly flour the rolling surface and rolling pin. Roll the remaining piece of dough into a rectangle about 12 by 8 inches and $1/4$ inch thick. Slide a thin metal spatula under the dough to loosen it from the rolling surface, then use an 8-inch-long gingerbread person cookie cutter to cut out 2 people. Carefully fold the arms over the chest of each and slide the cookies onto the baking sheet, placing them about 2 inches apart. Open out the arms. Press the scraps together, wrap them in plastic wrap, and set aside. Unwrap the second piece of dough and repeat the rolling and cutting process. Transfer the cookies to the baking sheet. Gather together all of the dough scraps, forming a smooth disk. Repeat the rolling and cutting process, but roll the scraps to an 18-by-8-inch rectangle and cut out 3 cookies. Repeat the rolling and cutting process, this time rolling to a 12-by-8 inch rectangle again to make 2 cookies, for a total of 9 cookies. Firmly press raisins into each cookie to form eyes, a nose, and a mouth and to make 3 or 4 buttons down the middle of the body.

Bake one sheet at a time until the cookies feel firm on top, about 12 minutes. The cookies will puff and thicken slightly during baking but not spread much. Cool the cookies for 5 minutes on the baking sheets, then use a wide metal spatula to transfer them to a wire rack to cool completely. If desired, while the cookies are still warm, you can use a toothpick to poke a hole in the top of each one so that it can be hung as an ornament.

MAKE THE FROSTING. In a small bowl, stir the powdered sugar together with enough cream to form a thick, firm frosting. Spoon the frosting into a small pastry bag fitted with a small round writing tip or a plastic freezer bag with a tiny hole cut in one corner. Holding the pastry tip or plastic bag about 1 inch above the cookie and moving it slowly, pipe hair, a mouth, shoes, and whatever else you like for decoration on each cookie. Draw a frosting bow or bow tie at the neck, or outline a dress or jacket. Or create any whimsical design you choose. (Sometimes I look at pictures of decorated gingerbread cookies for ideas.) Let the cookies sit until the frosting is firm.

The cookies can be layered between sheets of wax paper in a tightly sealed container and stored at room temperature for up to 3 weeks. The flavor improves the day after baking.

makes 9 cookies • **cookie making** 30 minutes (including decorating)
cookie baking 325 degrees, two baking sheets for about 12 minutes each

big-hearted butter shortbread

Shortbread is easy to love. The ingredients are simple, it is fast to mix and easy to roll, and its chief flavor is butter, pure butter. In baking, the term "short" refers to a dough that has a large proportion of fat (read butter) to flour. The cornstarch that replaces some of the flour in this version lowers the gluten content of the dough and makes the cookies especially tender. I like to cut the dough into perfect hearts, but trees, shamrocks, bells, and stars are other good possibilities.

cookies

1 3/4	cups unbleached all-purpose flour
1/4	cup cornstarch
1/2	teaspoon baking powder
1/4	teaspoon salt
1	cup (2 sticks) cold unsalted butter
3/4	cup powdered sugar
2	teaspoons vanilla extract

powdered sugar glaze

1 1/2	cups powdered sugar
1/2	teaspoon vanilla extract
5 to 6	tablespoons heavy (whipping) cream

Position a rack in the middle of the oven. Preheat the oven to 325 degrees F. Line one baking sheet if making 9 cookies, or two baking sheets if making 13 cookies, with parchment paper.

MAKE THE COOKIES. Sift the flour, cornstarch, baking powder, and salt into a medium bowl and set aside. In a large bowl, using an electric mixer on medium speed, beat the butter, powdered sugar, and vanilla until smooth and creamy, about 1 minute. Stop the mixer and scrape the sides of the bowl as needed during mixing. On low speed, add the flour mixture, mixing until it is incorporated and the dough holds together in large clumps and comes away from the sides of the bowl.

Form the dough into a smooth ball. Lightly flour the rolling surface and rolling pin. Roll the dough out to a $1/4$-inch thickness. Using a 4 $1/2$- or 3 $1/2$-inch-long heart-shaped cutter, cut out the hearts. Use a thin metal spatula to transfer them to the prepared baking sheets, placing them about 1 inch apart. Gather together the dough scraps, roll them, and cut out additional hearts.

Bake one sheet at a time until the edges and bottoms of the cookies are lightly browned, about 20 minutes. Cool the cookies on the baking sheet for 5 minutes, then use a wide metal spatula to transfer them to a wire rack to cool completely.

recipe continued next page

MAKE THE GLAZE. In a small bowl, stir the powdered sugar and vanilla together with enough cream to form a thick, spreadable glaze. Use a thin metal spatula to spread half of each cookie heart with glaze. Let the cookies sit until the glaze is firm.

The cookies can be layered between sheets of wax paper in a tightly covered container and stored at room temperature for up to 4 days.

choices

Flavorings such as 1 teaspoon finely grated lemon zest, 2 teaspoons finely grated orange zest, or 3/4 teaspoon almond extract can be added to the dough along with the vanilla. The cookies can be half-dipped in semisweet Chocolate Coating (page 47) rather than spread with the vanilla glaze. Or make a double recipe of the glaze and cover the tops of the cookies entirely.

makes nine 4 1/2-inch-long hearts or thirteen 3 1/2-inch-long hearts · **cookie making** 20 minutes

cookie baking 325 degrees, one baking sheet for 9 larger cookies or two baking sheets for 13 smaller cookies, for about 20 minutes each

toasted **coconut** washboards

●●●

These rectangular cookies mimic the shape and ridged texture of an old-fashioned washboard. Toasted coconut adds crunch to the crisp cookies and decorates the white-chocolate-dipped ends. Drawing the tines of a fork down the length of the unbaked cookies makes the characteristic ridges, but be sure to hold the fork so that its underside faces down to produce smooth, even ridges. This is a sticky dough, so it's easiest to roll it out between two pieces of wax paper.

2 cups (about 6 ounces) sweetened shredded coconut
2 cups unbleached all-purpose flour
³/₄ teaspoon baking powder
¹/₈ teaspoon salt
¹/₂ teaspoon ground cinnamon
³/₄ cup (1 ¹/₂ sticks) unsalted butter, at room temperature
1 cup packed light brown sugar
1 large egg
1 teaspoon vanilla extract
¹/₂ teaspoon almond extract

2 ounces white chocolate, chopped

Position a rack in the middle of the oven. Preheat the oven to 300 degrees F.

Spread the coconut on a baking sheet. Bake for about 10 minutes, stirring once, until the coconut becomes evenly golden. Watch carefully, as the coconut can darken quickly toward the end of baking. Set aside to cool. Increase the oven temperature to 350 degrees F. Line two baking sheets with parchment paper.

Sift the flour, baking powder, salt, and cinnamon into a medium bowl and set aside.

In a large bowl, using an electric mixer on medium speed, beat the butter and brown sugar until smooth and fluffy, about 1 minute. Stop the mixer and scrape the sides of the bowl as needed during mixing. Add the egg, vanilla, and almond extract and mix until blended, about 1 minute. On low speed, add the flour mixture, mixing just until it is incorporated. Use a large spoon to stir in 1 ¹/₂ cups of the toasted coconut.

Divide the dough into 2 portions and pat each into a flat rectangle. Cut 2 large sheets of wax paper, and roll one portion of dough between the wax paper into a 7 ¹/₂-by-12-inch rectangle that is about ¹/₄ inch thick. Remove the top piece of wax paper and discard it. Trim the edges of the dough slightly to even them. Cut the dough into 9 rectangles that measure about 4 by 2 ¹/₂ inches. Lift the

. . . . recipe continued next page cookies, on the wax paper, and place cookie side down on a prepared baking sheet. Lift off the wax paper and use a metal spatula to separate and spread out the cookies so they are about 2 inches apart. Holding a fork so the underside is facing down, draw the tines of the fork down the length of each cookie to cover it with parallel lines. Repeat with the second rectangle of dough.

Bake one sheet at a time until the edges and bottoms of the cookies are lightly browned, about 15 minutes. The centers should remain light in color. Cool the cookies for 5 minutes on the baking sheets, then use a wide metal spatula to transfer them to a wire rack to cool completely.

Put the white chocolate in a heatproof container or top of a double boiler, and place it over, but not touching, a saucepan of barely simmering water (or the bottom of the double boiler). Stir until melted and smooth. Remove from the water and let the white chocolate cool and thicken slightly, about 10 minutes.

Use a pastry brush to paint a 1-inch border of melted white chocolate across one narrow end of each cookie. Sprinkle the remaining toasted coconut on the white chocolate. Let the cookies sit at room temperature until the white chocolate is firm, about 1 hour. Or, to speed the firming of the white chocolate, refrigerate the cookies uncovered for about 15 minutes, then remove from the refrigerator.

The cookies can be individually wrapped in plastic wrap and stored at room temperature for up to 3 days.

makes 18 cookies · **cookie making** 25 minutes · **cookie baking** 350 degrees, two baking sheets for about 15 minutes each

lemon butter **crumb** cookies

More crumbs, more crumbs, I always think whenever I eat a crumb-topped cake, pie, or crisp. These cookies, made from a lemon-flavored crumb topping mixture, are nothing but crumbs. As they bake, the butter in the crumb mixture melts and the crumbs become crisp cookies that have as many crumbs as anyone could want, even me. Orange zest is another option for flavoring them.

1 cup (2 sticks) unsalted butter, at room temperature
1 cup sugar
1/8 teaspoon salt
2 teaspoons finely grated lemon zest
2 teaspoons vanilla extract
3 cups unbleached all-purpose flour

Powdered sugar for dusting

Position a rack in the middle of the oven. Preheat the oven to 325 degrees F. Trace nine 3 1/2-inch circles on each of two pieces of parchment paper the size of your baking sheets, leaving 1 inch between the circles. Line the baking sheets with the paper, marked side down.

In a large bowl, using an electric mixer on low speed, beat the butter, sugar, salt, lemon zest, and vanilla until smoothly blended, about 1 minute. Stop the mixer and scrape the sides of the bowl as needed during mixing. Add the flour and mix until the dough forms small crumbs, varying in size from fine crumbs to about 1/4 inch in size.

Use a 1/4-cup measuring cup to scoop up 1/4 cup crumbs, and spread them in one of the marked circles. Pat the crumbs gently to fill the circle, but do not pack them tightly. Sprinkle about 1 tablespoon of loose crumbs over the top, to produce the crumbly looking top. Repeat to make a total of 18 cookies.

Bake the cookies one sheet at a time until the bottoms and edges are light brown, about 21 minutes. The centers of the cookies should still be a lighter pale golden color. Cool the cookies for 10 minutes on the baking sheets, then use a wide metal spatula to transfer them to a wire rack to cool completely (some crumbs may fall off the edges). Do not try to transfer the cookies before 10 minutes—they must cool and firm slightly so they will not break.

Dust the cooled cookies lightly with powdered sugar. The cookies can be stored in a tightly covered container at room temperature for up to 3 days.

makes 18 cookies · **cookie making** 15 minutes · **cookie baking** 325 degrees, two baking sheets for about 21 minutes each

super-sized **butter pecan** meltaways

These are the large version of those tender nutty cookies coated in powdered sugar that are often called Mexican wedding cookies or Russian tea cookies. This is also the slice–and–bake fast version. The square cookies are quickly cut from a chilled block of dough. A food processor—mini or regular size—works well for grinding the pecans.

2	cups unbleached all-purpose flour
1	teaspoon baking powder
1/2	teaspoon salt
1/2	teaspoon ground cinnamon
1	cup (2 sticks) unsalted butter, at room temperature
1/2	cup powdered sugar, plus **3** tablespoons for dusting
2	teaspoons vanilla extract
1 1/2	cups (about 6 ounces) finely ground pecans

Sift the flour, baking powder, salt, and cinnamon into a medium bowl and set aside. In a large bowl, using an electric mixer on medium speed, beat the butter, $1/2$ cup powdered sugar, and vanilla until smoothly blended, about 1 minute. Stop the mixer and scrape the sides of the bowl as needed during mixing. On low speed, add the flour mixture, mixing just until it is incorporated and the dough looks smooth. Mix in the pecans until thoroughly blended.

Form the dough into a 6-by-2 $1/2$-by-2 $1/2$-inch block. Wrap it in plastic wrap and refrigerate for at least 3 hours, or overnight, until it is cold and firm.

Position a rack in the middle of the oven. Preheat the oven to 325 degrees F. Line two baking sheets with parchment paper.

Unwrap the cold dough. Use a large sharp knife to cut the dough into eighteen $1/3$-inch-thick slices. Place the cookies 1 inch apart on the prepared baking sheets. (These cookies do not spread a lot.)

Bake one sheet at a time until the edges and bottoms are lightly browned, about 23 minutes. Cool the cookies for 5 minutes on the baking sheets, then use a wide metal spatula to transfer them to a wire rack to cool completely.

Push the cookies close together on the rack. Sift the 3 tablespoons powdered sugar over the tops to coat them lightly but evenly.

The cookies can be stored in a tightly covered container at room temperature for up to 3 days.

makes 18 cookies ▪ **cookie making** 15 minutes ▪ **cookie baking** 325 degrees, two baking sheets for about 23 minutes each

oatmeal **trailblazers**

These cookies can travel. Whether you are hiking a trail, biking the quiet roads, or flying across the country, Oatmeal Trailblazers, studded with dried fruit and nuts, will keep you going over the last hill or get you happily to your final destination. The soft dough is rolled into balls, then rolled in a bowl of trail mix. The fruit and nuts cling to the soft dough, so that each baked cookie has its top and bottom coated with more than 2 1/2 tablespoons of trail mix. Definitely a cookie pick-me-up.

I use a trail mix that has a good selection of dried fruit and nuts. If there are any large pieces of fruit or whole nuts, I cut them into small pieces. Sometimes I add my favorite dried fruits or nuts, such as pecans, walnuts, sunflower seeds, or apricot pieces, to the basic mix. During baking, the nuts toast and the dried fruits become pleasantly chewy. The flavor of these cookies changes with each bite as you taste a different fruit or nut.

2	cups unbleached all-purpose flour
1	teaspoon baking soda
3/4	teaspoon baking powder
1/2	teaspoon salt
1 1/2	teaspoons ground cinnamon
1	cup (2 sticks) unsalted butter, at room temperature
1	cup granulated sugar
1	cup packed light brown sugar
2	large eggs
2	teaspoons vanilla extract
2 1/2	cups oatmeal (not quick-cooking)
2 1/2	cups (about 12 ounces) fruit and nut trail mix, pieces no larger than 1/2 inch

Position a rack in the middle of the oven. Preheat the oven to 325 degrees F. Line two baking sheets with parchment paper.

In a medium bowl, stir the flour, baking soda, baking powder, salt, and cinnamon together; set aside. In a large bowl, using an electric mixer on medium speed, beat the butter, granulated sugar, and brown sugar until smoothly blended, about 1 minute. Stop the mixer and scrape the sides of the bowl as needed during mixing. Add the eggs and vanilla and mix until blended, about 1 minute. On low speed, add the flour mixture, mixing just until it is incorporated. Mix in the oatmeal.

Put the trail mix in a medium bowl.

Using an ice cream scoop or measuring cup with a $1/4$-cup capacity, scoop out portions of dough and roll each one between the palms of your hands into a ball. Roll each ball around in the fruit and nut mix to coat it thickly with the mix, and place the cookie balls on the prepared baking sheets, spacing them 3 inches apart.

Bake the cookies one sheet at a time until the bottoms and edges are light brown, about 23 minutes. As the cookies bake and flatten, the fruit and nuts will spread out over the cookies. Cool the cookies for 5 minutes on the baking sheets, then use a wide metal spatula to transfer them to a wire rack to cool completely.

The cookies can be stored in a tightly covered container at room temperature for up to 5 days.

choices

To freeze the cooled cookies and have them ready for trips, wrap them tightly in plastic wrap and put them in a tightly covered metal or plastic freezer container. Label with the date and contents and freeze for up to 3 months. Remove as many cookies from the freezer as needed and defrost the still-wrapped cookies at room temperature.

makes 15 cookies • **cookie making** 15 minutes • **cookie baking** 325 degrees, two baking sheets for about 23 minutes each

pine nut and fig **roundups**

● ●

Bumps are a good characteristic in these cookies: they signal that there are lots of chewy pieces of dried figs buried in them. The top of each cookie is covered with a thick layer of pine nuts that toasts to a golden color as the cookies bake. Blanched slivered almonds can be substituted for the pine nuts.

1 1/4 cups unbleached all-purpose flour
  1/4 teaspoon salt
    1 teaspoon ground cinnamon
  3/4 cup (1 1/2 sticks) unsalted butter,
      at room temperature
  2/3 cup packed light brown sugar
    1 cup (about 4 ounces) dried figs,
      cut into 1/2-inch pieces
  3/4 cup (about 3 1/2 ounces) pine nuts,
      not toasted

Position a rack in the middle of the oven. Preheat the oven to 325 degrees F. Line a baking sheet with parchment paper.

Sift the flour, salt, and cinnamon into a medium bowl and set aside. In a large bowl, using an electric mixer on medium speed, beat the butter and brown sugar until the color lightens and the mixture looks smooth, about 1 minute. Stop the mixer and scrape the sides of the bowl as needed during mixing. On low speed, add the flour mixture, mixing until a smooth dough forms. Stir in the figs.

Using a heaping tablespoon (about 3 level tablespoons each) of dough for each cookie, roll the dough between the palms of your hands into smooth balls. Use the palm of your hand to flatten each cookie into a 3-inch disk and place them 1 inch apart on the prepared baking sheet. (These cookies do not spread much.) Sprinkle the pine nuts thickly over the top of the cookies, pressing them gently into the dough; use about 40 pine nuts for each cookie.

Bake until the edges of the cookies brown lightly and the pine nuts are lightly toasted, about 20 minutes. Cool the cookies for 5 minutes on the baking sheet, then use a wide metal spatula to transfer them to a wire cake rack to cool completely. The cookies will become crisp as they cool.

The cookies can be stored in a tightly covered container at room temperature for up to 3 days.

makes 12 cookies · **cookie making** 15 minutes · **cookie baking** 325 degrees, for about 20 minutes

jumbo almond **elephant ears**

"Are you making those elephant ears again?" my husband asked as I filled the freezer with batches of delicious, but not large, flaky cookies. To make these cookies jumbo-sized, I thought that all I'd have to do would be to roll up huge sheets of dough into a double spiral shape. No such luck—until I had a brainstorm. I rolled out a rectangle of dough, spread it with filling, and rolled it into a double spiral—elephant ear—shape. Then I cut the log of dough into thick slices and rolled each slice again to flatten it into a large cookie. Eureka. It was the solution to making large (5-by-6-inch) butterfly-shaped cookies. To prevent sticking as you roll the dough, sprinkle it generously with sugar. As the cookies bake, this sugar caramelizes and forms a crisp bubbly sugar coating .

These elephant ears are made with a quick sour cream dough that resembles tender, buttery puff pastry.

Almond paste is a finely ground mixture of almonds and sugar found in the baking section of most supermarkets.

cookie dough

2	cups unbleached all-purpose flour
1	teaspoon baking soda
1/2	teaspoon salt
1	cup (2 sticks) cold unsalted butter, cut into 1/2-inch pieces
1/2	cup sour cream

filling

7	ounces almond paste, broken or cut into 12 pieces
2	tablespoons unsalted butter, at room temperature
3/4	cup powdered sugar
2	teaspoons heavy (whipping) cream or milk
1/2	teaspoon vanilla extract
1	teaspoon almond extract

about 1 cup granulated sugar for rolling

PREPARE THE DOUGH. Sift the flour, baking soda, and salt into a large bowl. Add the butter and mix with an electric mixer on low speed until the largest of the butter pieces are the size of small lima beans, about 20 seconds. The butter pieces will be different sizes, and there will still be some loose flour. Add the sour cream and mix until large clumps of dough form that pull away from the sides of the bowl, about 15 seconds. (Or, use a pastry blender to combine the flour mixture and butter. Add the sour cream and stir with a large spoon for about 2 minutes until a smooth dough forms.) Form the dough into a smooth ball and flatten it into a rectangle about 8 by 5 inches. You will see small pieces of butter in the dough; that is good and contributes to the flaky texture. Wrap in plastic wrap and refrigerate for 30 to 60 minutes to rest and firm the dough. The dough can also be refrigerated overnight, but then it will have to sit at room temperature until it is soft enough to roll out easily—this can take as long as 1 hour in a cool kitchen.

PREPARE THE FILLING. In a large bowl, using an electric mixer on medium speed, beat the almond paste and butter until smooth. Mix in the powdered sugar, cream or milk, vanilla, and almond extract until blended to a smooth soft mixture. (Or, make the filling in a food processor. Put all of the ingredients in the processor and, beginning with a few on/off bursts, process until a smooth mixture forms, about 1 minute.) Transfer to a small bowl, cover, and set aside at room temperature for up to 1 hour or refrigerate if leaving overnight.

Position a rack in the middle of the oven. Preheat the oven to 375 degrees F. Line two baking sheets with parchment paper.

Unwrap the dough. Lightly sprinkle flour and sugar on the rolling pin and rolling surface. Roll the dough to a 14-by-12-inch rectangle. Don't flip the dough over while rolling, but lift and turn it several times as you roll it to prevent it from sticking to the rolling surface. And when you lift and turn the dough, sprinkle sugar generously on the rolling surface. Use a thin metal spatula to spread the filling in a thin layer over the dough. Turn the dough if necessary so a short side faces you.

Measuring along the 14-inch sides, mark the center of the dough. Rolling from the shorter 12-inch edge that is closer to you, roll up the dough like a jelly roll just to the marked center. Then roll the far side toward the center until the two rolls meet. You will have a double log of filled dough that is smoothly attached on the bottom side. Turn the double log over for easier cutting.

Press in the ends of the log to smooth them, and use a large sharp knife to cut the log into twelve 1-inch-thick slices. Dip both sides of each slice in sugar. Sprinkle the rolling pin with sugar. Roll out each slice of dough to a large butterfly shape about 4 by 5 inches and about $^3/_{16}$ inch thick, sprinkling the rolling pin as necessary with sugar. The cookies will not all be exactly the same size. Use a large spatula to place the cookies at least 1 inch apart on the prepared baking sheets. Sprinkle the top of each cookie with about $^1/_2$ teaspoon sugar.

Bake the cookies one sheet at a time until the tops are evenly light brown, about 15 minutes. The cookies will spread about 1 inch and rise slightly. The filling may bubble up slightly on some of the cookies and have a few darker spots. Cool the cookies for 5 minutes on the baking sheets, then use a large metal spatula to carefully transfer them to a wire rack to cool completely. The outsides of the sugar-coated cookies will become very crisp as they cool.

The cookies can be stored in a single layer in a tightly covered container at room temperature for up to 3 days.

makes 12 cookies • **cookie making** 35 minutes • **cookie baking** 375 degrees, two baking sheets for about 15 minutes each

cornmeal currant **crunch** cookies

Several years ago, my husband and I spent Easter week in the Italian village of San Gimignano. Each morning we woke to a deserted village, but by afternoon, the pedestrian streets were impassable with visitors. I know they came to see the famous towers, but I think many also came to buy the golden cornmeal cookies from the little bakery across from our hotel. The super–crunchy cookies were piled in huge bins that held cookies with nuts, apricots, or currants. My favorite was the one with little bits of chewy currants and crisp nuts.

1 1/2   cups unbleached all-purpose flour
1/2   cup yellow cornmeal
1   teaspoon baking powder
1/4   teaspoon salt
3/4   cup (1 1/2 sticks) unsalted butter, at room temperature
3/4   cup plus **3** tablespoons sugar
1   teaspoon finely grated lemon zest
2   large egg yolks
1   teaspoon vanilla extract
1/2   cup dried currants
1/2   cup chopped pecans, plus
14   pecan halves (optional)

Position a rack in the middle of the oven. Preheat the oven to 350 degrees F. Line two baking sheets with parchment paper.

In a medium bowl, stir the flour, cornmeal, baking powder, and salt together; set aside. In a large bowl, using an electric mixer on medium speed, beat the butter, 3/4 cup of the sugar, and the lemon zest until smooth and creamy and the color has lightened slightly, about 1 minute. Stop the mixer and scrape the sides of the bowl as needed during mixing. Add the egg yolks and vanilla and mix until blended, about 1 minute. On low speed, add the flour mixture, mixing just until it is incorporated. Mix in the currants and chopped pecans.

Spread the remaining 3 tablespoons sugar on a large piece of parchment or wax paper. Using an ice cream scoop or measuring cup with a $1/4$-cup capacity, scoop out portions of dough. Roll each one between the palms of your hands into a smooth ball, then roll each ball in the sugar, flatten it to about a 3 $1/2$-inch circle, and place the cookies 2 inches apart on the baking sheets. Press a pecan half into the center of each cookie, if desired.

Bake one sheet at a time until the bottoms and edges are lightly browned, about 15 minutes. Cool the cookies for 5 minutes on the baking sheets, then use a wide metal spatula to transfer them to a wire rack to cool completely.

The cookies can be stored in a tightly covered container at room temperature for up to 3 days.

makes 14 cookies • **cookie making** 15 minutes • **cookie baking** 350 degrees, two baking sheets for about 15 minutes each

peanut-covered **peanut butter** cookie slabs

The dough for these cookies is formed into a large slab, chilled, and then sliced into nice uniform smaller slabs for baking. The slice–and–bake method eliminates rolling out a dough and is a fast way to form cookies. Once the dough slab is cold and firm, it is easy to cut into neat, even slices. Vary the thickness of the cookies as you like by cutting thicker or thinner slices. You can refrigerate the dough for as long as overnight before making cookies, or freeze it for up to 1 month and bake it whenever you want. Defrost the dough in the refrigerator for at least 8 hours, or overnight. (Cold dough slices easily, but frozen dough has a tendency to crumble.) The cookies spread to an oval shape during baking. Since both the peanut butter and the peanuts include salt, there is no salt added to the dough.

1 ½	cups unbleached all-purpose flour
½	teaspoon baking soda
½	cup (1 stick) unsalted butter, at room temperature
½	cup smooth peanut butter, at room temperature
½	cup granulated sugar
⅓	cup packed light brown sugar
1	large egg
1	teaspoon vanilla extract
1	cup coarsely chopped lightly salted peanuts

Sift the flour and baking soda into a medium bowl and set aside. In a large bowl, using an electric mixer on medium speed, beat the butter and peanut butter just to blend them together. Stop the mixer and scrape the sides of the bowl as needed during mixing. Add the granulated sugar and brown sugar and beat until smoothly blended, about 30 seconds. Add the egg and vanilla and mix until thoroughly blended, about 1 minute. On low speed, add the flour mixture, mixing just until it is incorporated.

Form the dough into a rough 5-by-3-by-2 ½-inch rectangular slab. Wrap in plastic wrap and refrigerate to firm the dough slightly, about 30 minutes.

Shape the rectangle again and rewrap it. (This makes the shape more defined.) Refrigerate the dough for at least 3 hours, or overnight, until it is cold and firm. Or wrap it tightly and freeze it for up to 1 month; thaw in the refrigerator before using.

Position a rack in the middle of the oven. Preheat the oven to 350 degrees F. Line two baking sheets with parchment paper.

recipe continued next page

Unwrap the cold dough. Use a large sharp knife to cut the dough into fifteen $^1/_3$-inch-thick slices, and place the cookies 3 inches apart on the prepared baking sheets. Sprinkle about 1 tablespoon of the chopped peanuts evenly over the top of each cookie, and press the peanuts gently but firmly into the dough. This pressing will make the cookies spread about an additional $^1/_2$ inch.

Bake one sheet at a time until the edges and bottoms are lightly browned, about 14 minutes. Cool the cookies for 5 minutes on the baking sheets, then use a wide metal spatula to transfer them to a wire rack to cool completely. Serve at room temperature.

The cookies can be stored in a tightly covered container at room temperature for up to 3 days.

makes 15 cookies • **cookie making** 15 minutes • **cookie baking** 350 degrees, two baking sheets for about 14 minutes each

long, tall **apricot almond** biscotti

Our friend Alan Roberts may have come to baking later in life, but his enthusiasm has made up for any late start. He is now the official "bringer of desserts" for every gathering of his large extended family. Alan's most recent creation is a crisp biscotti that is studded with dried apricots and whole almonds. For this long biscotti, he slices logs of partially baked dough lengthwise into long strips, then bakes them again at a low temperature to make them crisp. Alan notes that it is easy to cut through the whole nuts as long as the cookie logs are still warm.

Walnuts and pecans can substitute for the almonds, and dried cranberries, raisins, or date pieces can substitute for the apricots. Biscotti make great dunking cookies with tea or coffee.

1 cup (about 5 ounces) whole unblanched (with skins) almonds

2 cups unbleached all-purpose flour

1 teaspoon baking powder

1/4 teaspoon salt

3/4 cup packed light brown sugar

5 tablespoons cold unsalted butter, cut into 1/2-inch or smaller pieces

1 large egg, plus **1** large egg yolk beaten with **1** tablespoon water, for egg wash

1/3 cup whole milk

1/2 teaspoon vanilla extract

1/4 teaspoon almond extract

1 cup (4 ounces) dried apricots, cut into small pieces

Position a rack in the middle of the oven. Preheat the oven to 350 degrees F.

Spread the almonds on a baking sheet and bake for 5 minutes. Transfer the almonds to a small bowl and set aside to cool. Line the baking sheet with parchment paper.

In a large bowl, use a fork to stir together the flour, baking powder, salt, and brown sugar until blended and any lumps of brown sugar disappear. Using the fork or your fingertips, mix in the butter pieces until small crumbs no larger than $1/2$ inch in size form.

In a small bowl, use the fork to beat the egg, milk, vanilla, and almond extract to blend them together and break up the yolk. Stir the liquids into the crumb mixture, then use your fingertips to form a smooth dough. Using a large spoon or your fingertips, mix in the almonds.

Divide the dough into 2 equal portions. On a lightly floured surface, pat one portion of dough into a 7-inch square. With the side of your hand, press an indentation about 2 inches wide down the center of the dough. Spread half of

recipe continued next page

the apricot pieces in the indentation. Fold the sides of the dough over to the center to enclose the apricots. Slide a large metal spatula under the log of dough to loosen it from the surface and then slide it onto the prepared baking sheet. Press down on the dough log to shape it into an 8-by-6-inch rectangle. Repeat with the remaining portion of dough; the shaped logs should be 2 inches apart on the sheet. Brush the tops lightly with the egg wash.

Bake until the edges brown and the tops feel firm and turn golden, about 20 minutes. Cool the partially baked cookie logs on the baking sheet on a wire rack for 20 minutes. Reduce the oven temperature to 300 degrees F.

Using a wide metal spatula, slide each log onto a cutting board. Use a large sharp knife to cut each log lengthwise into six 1-inch-wide slices. Line the baking sheet with clean parchment paper. Using a spatula to help move them, carefully return the cookie slices to the baking sheet, placing them 1 inch apart.

Bake for 30 minutes. Cool the biscotti for 5 minutes on the baking sheet, then carefully transfer them to a wire rack to cool thoroughly.

The biscotti can be stored in a tightly covered container at room temperature for up to 1 week.

makes 12 cookies • **cookie making** 20 minutes
cookie baking 350 degrees, for about 20 minutes; 300 degrees, for about 30 minutes

two-fisted**sandwich**cookies

When I was a kid, I always went for the sandwich cookies. Two cookies plus a filling— I knew a good deal when I saw it. When you want a cookie to be dessert, sandwich cookies fit the bill. Lemon-Ginger Cookie Sandwiches make perfect cookie tarts for an afternoon party, Lemon Whoopie Pies can star at a spring celebration, and Super-Fudge Brownie-Drop Ice Cream Sandwiches are a do-ahead grand finale.

Sandwich cookies have slightly longer ingredient lists than single cookies, but their fillings are all fast and simple, and these cookies are familiar and easy to make: they just look like something special. Quick frostings, chocolate and cream truffle fillings, jam, and ice cream provide a lot of filling choices.

All of these frosting, jam, fudge, and ice cream fillings can be mixed and matched with other cookies. Many of the soft or chewy cookies that appear earlier in the book can become sandwich versions. An essential quality for any great sandwich cookie is that it is not so thick or crisp that the filling squishes out when you try to eat it. Choose flavor pairings that you like

to create your own combinations. Fill Maple Cranberry Oatmeal Cookies or Pumpkin Butterscotch Chip Cookies with Cinnamon Cream Cheese Filling, for example, or Almond Butter Crisps with Lemon Cream Cheese Filling.

Sandwich cookies lend themselves to a two-step or do-ahead preparation. Make the cookies one day and fill them the next. Any of these sandwich cookies can be wrapped individually and frozen for up to a month. I find it reassuring to know a batch of these cookies is ready and waiting in my freezer. The single cookies can also be frozen and then filled before serving them.

With the exception of King-Sized Raisin Pillows, which have the layers sealed into one cookie, all of these cookies can stand alone as a single cookie without any filling.

I've kept the size of the cookies to four inches in diameter or less. Any larger, and a sandwich cookie becomes more than a normal serving. A nice way to serve several kinds of cookie sandwiches is to cut them into quarters. They make attractive wedges and give your guests the opportunity to try several varieties. Crisp cookie sandwiches, such as Almond Butter Crisps with Whipped Chocolate Truffle Filling and Lemon-Ginger Cookie Sandwiches are better left whole, however, since they may crumble if cut. Ice cream sandwiches cut easily and can be served with sundae sauces for dipping.

lemon **whoopie** pies

Whoopie pies are a New England specialty that combines two soft cake-like cookies held together by a thick layer of frosting. The traditional version is chocolate with white frosting, but I wanted to start a new tradition with lemon whoopie pies. The light, moist, soft cookies look like the top of a muffin. They are filled with a thick layer of lemon cream cheese frosting and they deserve a great big whoop of delight.

An average lemon yields about 2 teaspoons of zest (the yellow part of the peel) and 3 tablespoons of juice; be sure to grate the zest before squeezing the juice. This cake-like batter releases easily from the buttered parchment paper.

cookies

- **1 1/2** cups unbleached all-purpose flour
- **1/2** teaspoon baking powder
- **1/4** teaspoon baking soda
- **1/4** teaspoon salt
- **6** tablespoons ($^3/_4$ stick) unsalted butter, at room temperature
- **1** cup sugar
- **1** teaspoon finely grated lemon zest
- **1** large egg
- **1** tablespoon fresh lemon juice
- **1** teaspoon vanilla extract
- **1/2** cup buttermilk (any fat content is fine)

lemon cream cheese filling

- **6** tablespoons ($^3/_4$ stick) unsalted butter, at room temperature
- **6** ounces cream cheese, at room temperature
- **1** teaspoon vanilla extract
- **1** teaspoon finely grated lemon zest
- **2** tablespoons fresh lemon juice
- **2 $^3/_4$** cups powdered sugar

Position a rack in the middle of the oven. Preheat the oven to 350 degrees F. Line two baking sheets with parchment paper and butter the paper.

MAKE THE COOKIES. Sift the flour, baking powder, baking soda, and salt into a medium bowl and set aside. In a large bowl, using an electric mixer on medium speed, beat the butter, sugar, and lemon zest until smoothly blended, about 1 minute. Stop the mixer and scrape the sides of the bowl as needed during mixing. Add the egg, lemon juice, and vanilla, mixing until blended, about 1 minute. The batter may look curdled. On low speed, add half of the flour mixture, mixing just to incorporate it. Mix in the buttermilk. Mix in the remaining flour mixture just until it is incorporated and the batter looks smooth again.

Drop heaping tablespoons (about 3 level tablespoons each) of dough onto the prepared baking sheets, spacing them 3 inches apart. Bake the cookies one sheet at a time until a toothpick inserted in the center comes out clean and the tops feel firm, about 12 minutes. With the exception of a thin line at the edges, the tops of the cookies should not brown. Cool the cookies on the baking sheets for 10 minutes, then use a wide metal spatula to transfer them to a wire rack to cool completely.

MAKE THE FILLING. In a large bowl, using an electric mixer on low speed, beat the butter, cream cheese, vanilla, lemon zest, and lemon juice until thoroughly blended and smooth, about 1 minute. Add the powdered sugar and mix until smooth, about 1 minute. If the filling is too soft to hold its shape, refrigerate until it is firmer, about 30 minutes.

Turn half of the cookies bottom side up. Leaving a $^1/_4$-inch plain edge, use a thin metal spatula to spread each one with about $^1/_4$ cup of filling. (An ice cream scoop with a $^1/_4$-cup capacity makes quick work of this.) Gently press the flat bottoms of the remaining cookies onto the filling.

Wrap each cookie in plastic wrap and refrigerate for at least 1 hour. Serve cold. The wrapped cookies can be stored in the refrigerator for up to 4 days.

makes 8 cookie sandwiches · **cookie making** 25 minutes
cookie baking 350 degrees, two baking sheets for about 12 minutes each

toasted almond and **blueberry jam** cookie sandwiches

• •

The shape of these jam-filled almond cookie sandwiches is limited only by your choice of cookie cutters. Circles, rectangles, hearts, and stars are all good choices. No cookie cutters? Just cut the dough into neat rectangles or squares. The top cookie has a hole cut out of its center and is sprinkled with powdered sugar, so the bright jam shines through a white sugar-dusted top. Seedless raspberry, blackberry, or strawberry jam make other good filling choices. Rolling this soft dough between sheets of wax paper is an easy way to prevent it from sticking to the rolling surface.

2 cups unbleached all-purpose flour

1/2 teaspoon salt

1 cup (2 sticks) unsalted butter, at room temperature

3/4 cup powdered sugar, plus extra for dusting

1 teaspoon vanilla extract

3/4 teaspoon almond extract

1 cup (about 4 ounces) whole blanched almonds, toasted (see page 14) and finely ground

6 tablespoons blueberry jam

Sift the flour and salt into a medium bowl and set aside. In a large bowl, using an electric mixer on medium speed, beat the butter and 3/4 cup powdered sugar until smooth and slightly lightened in color, about 1 minute. Stop the mixer and scrape the sides of the bowl as needed during mixing. On low speed, mix in the vanilla, almond extract, and ground almonds. Mix in the flour mixture just until the flour is incorporated and the dough holds together.

Divide the dough in half and form into two 6-inch disks. Wrap each one in plastic wrap and refrigerate the dough until it is cold and firm enough to roll, about 40 minutes.

Preheat the oven to 325 degrees F. Line two baking sheets with parchment paper.

Remove one piece of dough from the refrigerator. Put the dough between 2 large sheets of wax paper and roll it into a rectangle about 12 by 8 inches and 1/4 inch thick. Remove the top piece of wax paper and discard it. Use a cookie cutter to cut out 3 1/2-inch circles (or any shape you like) from the dough, leaving the cookies on the wax paper. Turn the wax paper over, peel off the paper, and use a metal spatula to help place the circles 1 inch apart on one of the prepared baking sheets. (The cookies do not spread much.) Set aside the dough scraps. Using 2 clean pieces of wax paper, roll and cut the second piece of dough. Gather together all of the dough scraps, forming a smooth disk, and repeat the rolling and cutting process. You should have 20 cookies.

recipe continued next page

Cut a 1-inch circle (or other shape) from the center of half of the cookies and remove these circles from the cookies (the wide end of a pastry tube works well for cutting the circles). The dough "holes" can be baked along with the cookies for snacks.

Bake the cookies one sheet at a time until the edges are light brown and the tops firm, about 18 minutes. Cool the cookies for 5 minutes on the baking sheets, then use a wide metal spatula to transfer them to a wire rack to cool completely.

Turn the cookies without the holes bottom side up. Leaving a $^1/_4$-inch plain edge, spread a rounded teaspoon of jam over each one. Sift powdered sugar over the cookies with the holes and place them on top of the jam-covered cookies.

The cookie sandwiches can be stored in a tightly covered container at room temperature for up to 3 days.

makes 10 cookie sandwiches • **cookie making** 25 minutes plus chilling time
cookie baking 325 degrees, two baking sheets for about 18 minutes each

lemon-ginger cookie sandwiches

* *

Lemon zest packs a real punch when you want to add lemon flavor. These cookies and their filling get their powerful lemon flavor from the zest. Grate the lemon zest for the cookies and for the filling at the same time and keep it tightly covered until ready to use. A round cookie cutter with scalloped edges is a nice shape for these cookies, but heart, tree, or star cutters are also good choices.

cookies

2	cups unbleached all-purpose flour
1/2	teaspoon salt
2 1/2	teaspoons ground ginger
1	teaspoon ground cinnamon
1	cup (2 sticks) unsalted butter, at room temperature
1	cup powdered sugar
2	teaspoons finely grated lemon zest
1	teaspoon vanilla extract
1	cup (about 4 ounces) whole blanched almonds, toasted (see page 14) and finely ground

lemon filling

1/2	cup (1 stick) unsalted butter, at room temperature
1 1/2	cups powdered sugar
2	teaspoons finely grated lemon zest
1	tablespoon fresh lemon juice

MAKE THE COOKIES. Sift the flour, salt, ginger, and cinnamon into a medium bowl and set aside. In a large bowl, using an electric mixer on medium speed, beat the butter and powdered sugar until smooth and slightly lightened in color, about 1 minute. Stop the mixer and scrape the sides of the bowl as needed during mixing. On low speed, mix in the lemon zest, vanilla, and ground almonds. Mix in the flour mixture just until the flour is incorporated and the dough holds together and comes away from the sides of the bowl.

Divide the dough in half and form into two 6-inch disks. Wrap each one in plastic wrap and refrigerate the dough until it is cold and firm enough to roll, about 40 minutes.

Preheat the oven to 325 degrees F. Line two baking sheets with parchment paper.

Unwrap one piece of dough. Lightly flour the rolling surface and rolling pin. Roll the dough into a rectangle about 12 by 8 inches and $^1/_4$ inch thick. Slide a thin metal spatula under the dough to loosen it from the rolling surface. Use a round cookie cutter with scalloped edges to cut out 3 $^1/_4$- to 3 $^1/_2$-inch circles (or any shape you like) from the dough. Set the dough scraps aside. Use a metal spatula to place the circles 1 inch apart on one of the prepared baking sheets. (The cookies do not spread much.) Repeat the rolling and cutting process with the second piece of dough. Gather together all of the dough scraps, forming a smooth disk. Repeat the rolling and cutting process. You should have 18 cookies.

recipe continued next page

Cut a 1-inch circle (or other shape) from the center of half of the cookies and remove these circles from the cookies. (The wide end of a pastry tube works well for cutting the circles.) The dough "holes" can be baked along with the cookies for snacks.

Bake the cookies one sheet at a time until the edges are light brown and the tops firm, about 20 minutes. Cool the cookies for 5 minutes on the baking sheets, then use a wide metal spatula to transfer them to a wire rack to cool completely.

MAKE THE FILLING. In a medium bowl, using an electric mixer on medium speed, beat the butter, powdered sugar, lemon zest, and lemon juice until smooth.

Turn the cookies without the holes bottom side up. Leaving a $^1/_8$-inch plain edge, spread about 2 tablespoons of filling over each one. Place the bottoms of the cookies with the holes on top of the filling.

The cookie sandwiches can be wrapped individually in plastic wrap and stored in a tightly covered container in the refrigerator for up to 4 days. Bring to room temperature to serve.

makes 9 cookie sandwiches · **cookie making** 25 minutes plus chilling time
cookie baking 325 degrees, two baking sheets for about 20 minutes each

banana cream **double dates**

*When my friend Carole Emanuel tried these soft cookie sandwiches, she said they had an old–fashioned cookie flavor,
like those made by a grandmother. That describes them perfectly, right down to the cinnamon cream cheese filling.*

cookies

2	cups unbleached all-purpose flour
3/4	teaspoon baking powder
1/4	teaspoon salt
1	teaspoon ground cinnamon
1/2	cup (1 stick) unsalted butter, at room temperature
1/2	cup granulated sugar
1/2	cup packed light brown sugar
2	ripe bananas, peeled
1	large egg
1	teaspoon vanilla extract
1	cup (about 4 1/2 ounces) pitted dates, cut into 1/2- to 1/4-inch pieces

cinnamon cream cheese filling
(see lemon cream cheese filling, page 104, substituting 1 1/2 teaspoons of ground cinnamon for the lemon juice and zest)

Position a rack in the middle of the oven. Preheat the oven to 350 degrees F. Line two baking sheets with parchment paper and butter the paper.

MAKE THE COOKIES. Sift the flour, baking powder, salt, and cinnamon into a medium bowl and set aside. In a large bowl, using an electric mixer on low speed, beat the butter, granulated sugar, and brown sugar until smoothly blended, about 1 minute. Stop the mixer and scrape the sides of the bowl as needed during mixing. Break the bananas into about 1-inch pieces. Add the banana pieces and mix until just a few small pieces remain. The mixture will look curdled. Add the egg and vanilla and mix until blended, about 1 minute. Add the flour mixture, mixing just until it is incorporated and the batter looks smooth again. Mix in the dates.

Drop heaping tablespoons (about 3 level tablespoons each) of dough onto the prepared baking sheets, spacing them 3 inches apart. Use a small spatula to smooth the edges and tops, spreading them slightly to about 3/4 inch thick.

Bake the cookies one sheet at a time until the tops feel firm and a toothpick inserted in the center comes out clean, about 15 minutes. The cookie tops should not brown. Cool the cookies on the baking sheets for 5 minutes, then use a wide metal spatula to transfer them to a wire rack to cool completely.

Turn half of the cookies bottom side up. Use a thin metal spatula to spread a rounded tablespoon of filling over each one. Gently press the flat bottoms of the remaining cookies on top of the filling.

Wrap each cookie in plastic wrap and refrigerate for at least 1 hour. Serve cold. The wrapped cookies can be stored in the refrigerator for up to 4 days.

makes 8 cookie sandwiches · **cookie making** 25 minutes · **cookie baking** 350 degrees, two baking sheets for about 15 minutes each

peppermint **patties**

Two chocolate-covered chocolate wafers held together by a thick layer of peppermint-flavored frosting make a dessert cookie that could serve as the finale for the fanciest party or a refreshing ending to a spicy dinner. No party in the offing? These cookies are reason enough to party.

cookies

- **2** cups unbleached all-purpose flour
- **1/2** cup unsweetened Dutch-process cocoa powder
- **1/4** teaspoon baking soda
- **1/4** teaspoon salt
- **1** cup (2 sticks) unsalted butter, at room temperature
- **1** cup sugar
- **1** large egg
- **1** teaspoon vanilla extract

dark chocolate coating

- **6** ounces semisweet chocolate, chopped (1 cup)
- **1/2** ounce unsweetened chocolate, chopped
- **1 1/2** tablespoons canola or corn oil

peppermint filling

- **1/2** cup (1 stick) unsalted butter, at room temperature
- **2** cups powdered sugar
- **1** teaspoon vanilla extract
- **1/2** teaspoon peppermint extract

MAKE THE COOKIES. Sift the flour, cocoa powder, baking soda, and salt into a medium bowl and set aside. In a large bowl, using an electric mixer on low speed, beat the butter and sugar until blended and lightened in color, about 2 minutes. Stop the mixer and scrape the sides of the bowl as needed during mixing. Add the egg and vanilla and mix until blended, about 1 minute. On low speed, add the flour mixture, mixing just until it is incorporated and the batter looks smooth. Cover and refrigerate the dough for about 20 minutes to firm it slightly.

Position a rack in the middle of the oven. Preheat the oven to 325 degrees F. Line two baking sheets with parchment paper.

Roll heaping tablespoons (3 level tablespoons each) of dough between the palms of your hands into smooth 1 $^1/_2$-inch balls, and place them 3 $^1/_2$ inches apart on the prepared baking sheets. Using the palm of your hand, flatten the cookies to 2 $^1/_2$- to 3-inch rounds.

Bake the cookies one sheet at a time until the tops feel firm and look dull rather than shiny, about 15 minutes. Cool the cookies on the baking sheets for 5 minutes, then use a wide metal spatula to transfer them to a wire rack to cool completely.

. . . . recipe continued next page

MAKE THE CHOCOLATE COATING. Put both chocolates and the oil in a heatproof container or the top of a double boiler, and place it over, but not touching, a saucepan of barely simmering water (or the bottom of the double boiler). Stir until the chocolate is melted and smooth. Remove from the water and let the chocolate coating cool and thicken slightly, about 20 minutes.

Spoon the chocolate coating over the top of half of the cookies, using 1 tablespoon per cookie. Use the back of the spoon to spread the chocolate evenly and coat them completely. If some chocolate drizzles over the cookie edges, that is fine. (You will have about 2 tablespoons of the chocolate coating left for another use or to drizzle over ice cream.) Let the cookies sit at room temperature until the chocolate is firm. Or to speed the firming of the chocolate, refrigerate the cookies for about 20 minutes, then remove them from the refrigerator.

MAKE THE FILLING. In a large bowl, using an electric mixer on low speed, beat the butter, powdered sugar, vanilla, and peppermint extract until smoothly blended, about 1 minute. The filling will be quite thick. Turn the plain cookies bottom side up. Spoon a well-rounded tablespoon of filling into the center of each, carefully place the bottom of a chocolate-coated cookie on the frosting, and gently press the cookie to spread the filling into an even layer. The filling will not reach the edges.

Wrap each cookie in plastic wrap and refrigerate for at least 2 hours. Serve cold. The wrapped cookies can be stored in the refrigerator for up to 4 days.

choices

Coat all of the cookies with the chocolate coating and serve them as single chocolate cookies. Double the chocolate coating recipe (omit the peppermint filling).

makes 9 cookie sandwiches · **cookie making** 30 minutes, plus chilling time for the dough
cookie baking 325 degrees, two baking sheets for about 15 minutes each

king-sized **raisin** pillows

* *

Little pies or big cookies—whatever you call them, these "take anywhere" cookies are perfect for picnics, for sending off to a friend, or as a lunch box surprise. They have a raisin and brown sugar filling sandwiched between a fool-proof cream cheese pastry. The flaky pastry is so easy to handle that it even skips the rolling process—it can be patted into shape.

Be sure to cool the raisin filling before assembling the cookies, or the warm filling will melt the dough. There is no need to chill this dough before forming the cookies unless it's a hot summer day. Then the dough will be easier to handle if it is refrigerated briefly until it is firm.

filling
1 3/4	cups raisins
1/2	cup packed light brown sugar
1/2	cup water
1	tablespoon unbleached all-purpose flour
1/4	teaspoon ground nutmeg
1/2	teaspoon ground cinnamon

pastry
1	cup (2 sticks) unsalted butter, slightly softened (for about 30 minutes)
6	ounces cream cheese, slightly softened (for about 30 minutes)
1/8	teaspoon salt
1	cup unbleached all-purpose flour

icing
3/4	cup powdered sugar
1	tablespoon whole milk, plus up to 2 teaspoons if needed

Position a rack in the middle of the oven. Preheat the oven to 375 degrees F. Line a baking sheet with parchment paper.

MAKE THE FILLING. In a medium saucepan, combine the raisins, brown sugar, water, flour, nutmeg, and cinnamon and heat over medium heat, stirring often, until the brown sugar dissolves. Increase the heat to medium-high and bring to a boil. Reduce the heat and cook at a gentle boil for about 2 minutes, stirring occasionally, until the liquid is thick and syrupy. Set aside at room temperature until the mixture is cool to the touch, about 20 minutes. Once the raisins cool, they will look shiny and glazed.

MAKE THE PASTRY. In a large bowl, using an electric mixer on low speed, beat the butter, cream cheese, and salt until blended. Add the flour and continue mixing until a smooth dough forms.

Roll 2 tablespoons of the dough between the palms of your hands into a smooth ball. Press and flatten the dough to a 3 $1/2$-inch circle and place it on the prepared baking sheet; press down on it if necessary to make it the right size. Leaving a $1/4$-inch plain edge, spread 1 tablespoon of the cooled raisin filling over the dough. Press and flatten another 2 tablespoons of dough to a 3- to 3 $1/4$-inch circle.

Place the dough circle over the raisin filling and use a fork to seal the edges together. (The top circle is slightly smaller so that the dough edges are not overly thick.) Repeat to make a total of 12 cookies, spacing them 1 inch apart on the baking sheet.

Bake the cookies until the edges and bottoms are light brown, about 20 minutes. Cool the cookies on the baking sheet for 5 minutes, then use a wide metal spatula to transfer them to a wire rack to cool completely.

MAKE THE ICING. In a small bowl, stir the powdered sugar together with enough milk to form a thick but pourable icing. Leaving the edges plain, use a small metal spatula or dull knife to spread a thin layer of icing over the top of each cookie. Let the cookies sit at room temperature until the icing is firm.

The cookies can be stored in a tightly covered container at room temperature for up to 5 days.

choices

Omit the frosting. Before baking the cookies, use a pastry brush to brush the top of each with an egg wash made by beating 1 large egg together with 1 tablespoon heavy (whipping) cream. Sprinkle about $^1/_4$ teaspoon granulated sugar over the top of each cookie and bake as directed.

makes 12 cookie sandwiches • **cookie making** 25 minutes • **cookie baking** 375 degrees, for about 20 minutes

fudge-filled **chocolate chip cookie** sandwiches

My mother was famous in our family for her brown sugar chocolate chip cake. As many times as she made it during my childhood or shipped it to me at college, or that I have since made it for my family, it has remained a favorite of mine. Recently I realized that the thick batter could be turned into an outstanding soft chocolate chip cookie. The soft cookie is just right for holding a thick fudge filling. Mom would love it.

cookies

2	cups unbleached all-purpose flour
2	cups packed light brown sugar
1	teaspoon baking soda
1/2	cup (1 stick) cold unsalted butter, cut into pieces
1	large egg
1	teaspoon vanilla extract
1	cup sour cream
2	tablespoons whole milk
1 1/2	cups (9 ounces) semisweet chocolate chips

filling

1/2	cup heavy (whipping) cream
2	tablespoons unsalted butter, cut into pieces
1 1/3	cups (8 ounces) semisweet chocolate chips

Position a rack in the middle of the oven. Preheat the oven to 325 degrees F. Line two baking sheets with parchment paper and butter the paper.

MAKE THE COOKIES. In a large bowl, using an electric mixer on low speed, mix the flour, brown sugar, and baking soda to blend them. Add the butter and continue mixing until the butter pieces are the size of peas, about 2 minutes; you will still see some loose flour. Stop the mixer and scrape the sides of the bowl as needed during mixing. Mix in the egg and vanilla. The batter will still look dry. Mix in the sour cream and milk until the batter looks evenly moistened. You may still see lumps of butter. Mix in the chocolate chips.

Drop heaping tablespoons (about 3 level tablespoons each) of dough at least 2 1/2 inches apart onto the prepared baking sheets. Bake one sheet at a time until the tops feel soft but firm, the edges are lightly browned and crisp, and a toothpick inserted in the center comes out clean, about 17 minutes. (If the toothpick penetrates a chocolate chip, test another spot.)

Cool the cookies on the baking sheets for 10 minutes, then use a wide metal spatula to transfer them to a wire rack to cool completely.

recipe continued next page

MAKE THE FILLING. In a medium saucepan, heat the
cream and butter over low heat until the cream is hot
and the butter melts. The hot cream mixture should
form tiny bubbles and measure about 175 degrees F. on
a thermometer; do not let the mixture boil. Remove the
pan from the heat, add the chocolate chips, and let
them sit in the hot cream mixture for about 30 seconds
to soften. Whisk the filling until it is smooth and all of
the chocolate is melted.

Pour the chocolate filling into a medium bowl and let it
sit at room temperature until thickened enough to cling
to the cookies, about 45 minutes. Or, refrigerate it until
it thickens slightly, about 20 minutes.

Turn half of the cookies bottom side up. Leaving a
$^1/_8$-inch plain edge, spread the filling over the bottoms
of the cookies. If the filling is not thick and firm, let the
cookies sit until the it firms up before adding the top
cookie. Gently place the remaining cookies bottom side
down on top of the chocolate filling.

The cookies can be individually wrapped in plastic wrap
and stored in a tightly sealed tin at room temperature or
in the refrigerator for up to 3 days. Serve at room temperature or cold.

makes 12 cookie sandwiches • **cookie making** 20 minutes • **cookie baking** 325 degrees, two baking sheets for about 17 minutes each

almond butter crisps with whipped chocolate truffle filling

• •

It was Japan, of all places, that inspired these lace cookies with a thick and creamy chocolate filling. We were visiting my son in Tokyo, and I had heard that Wako was the best pastry shop in the city, so of course we made a trip to Ginza to check it out. Each pastry looked perfect, and every one we tried tasted as good as it looked, but there was one standout. I recognized it as a lace cookie that was made thick and not at all fragile by including a large pro-portion of nuts. The cookies were sandwiched together with a super-smooth chocolate filling.

These cookies look as sophisticated as those Asian cookies, but looks can be deceiving—in a good way. These are made from a one-pot batter that is dropped and baked to form perfectly round cookies, and the filling is as simple as melting chocolate chips in warm butter and cream.

The baking sheets should be lined so that the cookies can be removed easily. Either parchment paper or a non-stick liner, such as a Silpat, work well.

cookies

4 tablespoons (1/2 stick) unsalted butter
1/3 cup sugar
2 tablespoons light corn syrup
1/3 cup unbleached all-purpose flour
1 cup (about 4 ounces) finely ground blanched almonds
1 teaspoon vanilla extract
1/2 teaspoon almond extract

filling

6 tablespoons heavy (whipping) cream
1 tablespoon unsalted butter
1 cup (6 ounces) semisweet chocolate chips
1 teaspoon vanilla extract

Position a rack in the middle of the oven. Preheat the oven to 350 degrees F. Line two baking sheets with parchment paper or nonstick liners.

MAKE THE COOKIES. In a medium saucepan, cook the butter, sugar, and corn syrup over low heat, stirring often, until the butter melts and the sugar dissolves. Increase the heat to medium-high and bring to a boil, stirring constantly. The mixture will be smooth and syrupy. Remove the pan from the heat and stir in the flour to incorporate it. Stir in the ground almonds, vanilla, and almond extract. The batter will be thick.

Drop level tablespoons of batter 3 inches apart onto the prepared baking sheets. Use a dull knife to scrape the batter from the spoon if necessary. You should have 16 cookies.

Bake the cookies one sheet at a time until evenly light brown, about 11 minutes. After about 6 minutes of baking, the cookies will begin to bubble vigorously

....*recipe continued next page*

and then spread out. Cool the cookies on the baking sheets for 10 minutes, or until they are firm enough to move, then use a wide spatula to transfer them to a wire rack to cool completely (the cookies should slide easily off the baking liner). The cookies will become crisp as they cool.

MAKE THE FILLING. In a medium saucepan, heat the cream and butter over low heat until the cream is hot and the butter melts. The hot cream mixture should form tiny bubbles and measure about 175 degrees F. on a thermometer; do not let the mixture boil. Remove the pan from the heat, add the chocolate chips, and let them sit in the hot cream mixture for about 30 seconds to soften. Add the vanilla and whisk the filling until it is smooth and all of the chocolate has melted.

Pour the filling into a medium bowl and press plastic wrap onto the surface. Refrigerate until it is cold to the touch and just beginning to firm around the edges, about 30 minutes. Stir occasionally to ensure the mixture chills evenly.

Turn half of the cookies bottom side up. Use a whisk to beat the cold filling vigorously until it changes from a dark chocolate to a medium chocolate color and thickens slightly, about 30 seconds. Leaving a $1/4$-inch plain edge, immediately spread the whipped filling over the bottoms of the 8 cookies. Gently place the remaining cookies bottom side down on top of the filling. Let the cookies sit until the filling is firm, about 30 minutes.

Wrap each cookie in plastic wrap. The cookies can be stored at room temperature in a tightly sealed container for up to 3 days.

makes 8 cookie sandwiches · **cookie making** 20 minutes · **cookie baking** 350 degrees, two baking sheets for about 11 minutes each

super-fudge brownie-drop **ice cream** sandwiches

There is general agreement that ice cream and cookies are one of the world's perfect combinations. Put the two together in an ice cream sandwich and you add a do-way-ahead dimension. Brownie drop cookies are my cookie of choice. They can be sandwiched with any flavor of ice cream that goes well with chocolate (which in my opinion, includes every flavor except peach) and have such a soft fudgy texture that they do not become hard even when frozen. Chocolate chip cookie dough, coffee, peppermint, vanilla, or raspberry make especially good ice cream choices.

Many of the cookies in the "Big Chewy Cookies" chapter are also ideal ice cream sandwich candidates. For shape or flavor reasons, however, the Chocolate-Covered Chocolate Chip Cookie Mud Balls, Chocolate Caramel Pecan Clusters, Jumbo Black Bottom Coconut Macaroons, Morning Glory Breakfast Cookies, and Big City Black-and-Whites are the few cookies I would skip as an ice cream sandwich cookie. Chewy chocolate chip cookies make an especially great choice. A nice idea for a party is to make the sandwiches with a variety of ice cream flavors and let guests choose their favorite flavor.

For making any ice cream sandwich, the guidelines are the same. Let the cookies cool thoroughly before filling them. Letting the cooled cookies freeze for several hours is even better. Soften the ice cream (about 20 minutes in the refrigerator works well) just until it is spreadable but not melted, so the cookies do not become soggy. Wrap the ice cream sandwiches tightly and seal them tightly in a freezer storage container so they do not develop an "off" flavor or absorb odors. Give the wrapped ice cream sandwiches time to freeze firm before serving them. On a warm day, this can take at least 2 hours. Depending on the size of the cookie, plan on about $1/3$ to $1/2$ cup of ice cream for each sandwich.

1 $1/2$	cups (9 ounces) semisweet chocolate chips
$1/2$	cup (1 stick) unsalted butter, cut into pieces
1	teaspoon instant coffee, dissolved in **2** teaspoons water
2	large eggs
$3/4$	cup sugar
$1/8$	teaspoon salt
1	teaspoon vanilla extract
1	cup unbleached all-purpose flour
2	pints ice cream, softened just until spreadable

Position a rack in the middle of the oven. Preheat the oven to 350 degrees F. Line two baking sheets with parchment paper.

Put the chocolate chips, butter, and dissolved coffee in a heatproof container or the top of a double boiler and place it over, but not touching, a saucepan of barely simmering water (or the bottom of the double boiler). Stir the mixture until the chocolate chips and butter are melted and smooth. Remove from the water and set aside to cool slightly.

In a large bowl, using an electric mixer on medium speed, beat the eggs, sugar, salt, and vanilla until thickened and light yellow in color, about 2 minutes. Stop

......recipe continued next page

the mixer and scrape the sides of the bowl as needed during mixing. On low speed, mix in the melted chocolate mixture. Mix in the flour just until it is incorporated. Set the batter aside for 15 minutes to thicken slightly.

Using a measuring cup (which works best with this sticky batter) with a $^1/_4$-cup capacity, scoop up portions of batter and drop onto the prepared baking sheets, spacing the cookies 3 inches apart. Use a rubber spatula to scrape all of the batter from the measuring cup for each cookie.

Bake the cookies one sheet at a time until a toothpick inserted in the center of a cookie comes out with moist crumbs, not wet batter, clinging to it, about 13 minutes. Cool the cookies on the baking sheets for 5 minutes, then use a wide metal spatula to loosen the cookies from the parchment paper and transfer them to a wire rack to cool completely.

Wrap the cookies individually in plastic wrap and freeze them for at least 5 hours, or overnight.

Remove the cookies from the freezer and turn half of them bottom side up. Use a thin metal spatula to spread one cookie with about $^1/_3$ cup ice cream. Smooth the edges of the ice cream and top the ice cream with another cookie, flat side facing down, pressing the cookie gently onto the ice cream. Wrap the ice cream sandwich tightly in plastic wrap and freeze it. Continue filling and freezing the remaining cookies. (You will not use all of the ice cream.)

Freeze the ice cream sandwiches for at least 2 hours, or up to 1 week, before serving. For longer than overnight storage, seal the wrapped ice cream sandwiches in a clean container. Serve frozen.

makes 7 cookie sandwiches · **cookie making** 20 minutes · **cookie baking** 350 degrees, two baking sheets for about 13 minutes each

enjoy!

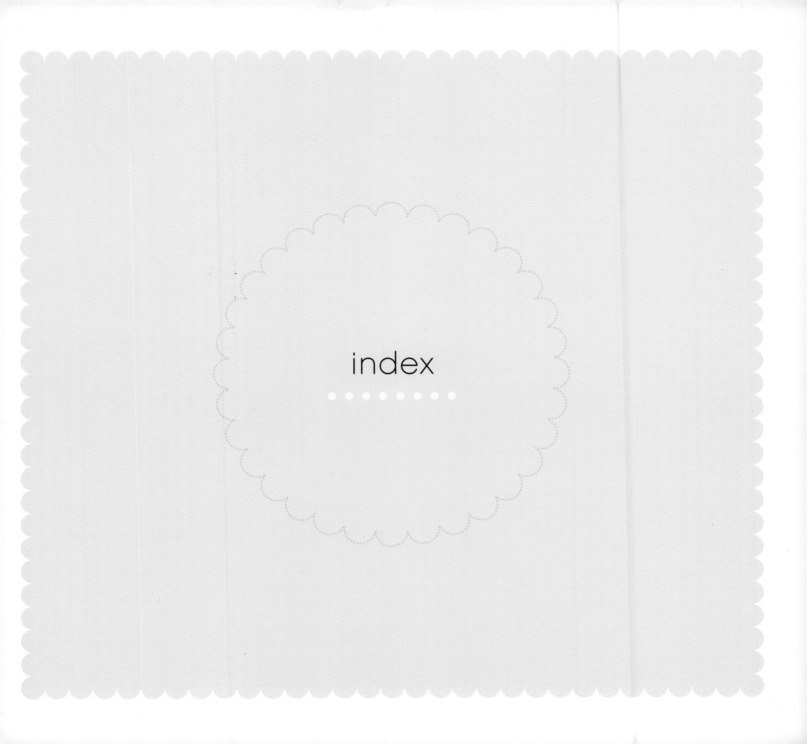

index

index

table**of**equivalents

The exact equivalents in the following tables have been rounded for convenience.

liquid/dry measures

u.s.	metric
$1/4$ teaspoon	1.25 milliliters
$1/2$ teaspoon	2.5 milliliters
1 teaspoon	5 milliliters
1 tablespoon (3 teaspoons)	15 milliliters
1 fluid ounce (2 tablespoons)	30 milliliters
$1/4$ cup	60 milliliters
$1/3$ cup	80 milliliters
$1/2$ cup	120 milliliters
1 cup	240 milliliters
1 pint (2 cups)	480 milliliters
1 quart (4 cups, 32 ounces)	960 milliliters
1 gallon (4 quarts)	3.84 liters
1 ounce (by weight)	28 grams
1 pound	454 grams
2.2 pounds	1 kilogram

length

u.s.	metric
$1/8$ inch	3 millimeters
$1/4$ inch	6 millimeters
$1/2$ inch	12 millimeters
1 inch	2.5 centimeters

oven temperature

fahrenheit	celsius	gas
250	120	$1/2$
275	140	1
300	150	2
325	160	3
350	180	4
375	190	5
400	200	6
425	220	7
450	230	8
475	240	9
500	260	10